THE OFFICIAL
PRISONER
COMPANION

THE OFFICIAL
PRISONER
COMPANION

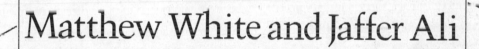

Matthew White and Jaffcr Ali

WARNER BOOKS

A Warner Communications Company

Warner gratefully acknowledges ITC Entertainment, Inc. for use of material from THE PRISONER, © 1967 ITC Incorporated Television Company Limited. All rights reserved.

Warner Books, Inc., 666 Fifth Avenue, New York, NY 10103

 A Warner Communications Company

Printed in the United States of America

First printing: July 1988

10 9 8 7 6 5 4

Library of Congress Cataloging in Publication Data
White, Matthew.
    The official Prisoner companion.

    1. Prisoner (Television program)   I. Ali, Jaffer.
II. Title.
PN1992.77.P7W47   1988   791.45′72   88-5606
ISBN 0-446-38744-4 (pbk.) (U.S.A.)

Book design: H. Roberts
Cover design by Suzanne Noli
Photographs courtesy of ITC Entertainment

CONTENTS

ACKNOWLEDGMENTS   *ix*

INTRODUCTION   *1*

Chapter One: PRISONER EPISODE GUIDE   *7*

   "Arrival"   *8*

   "The Chimes of Big Ben"   *15*

   "A. B. and C."   *22*

   "Free for All"   *28*

   "Schizoid Man"   *35*

   "The General"   *42*

   "Many Happy Returns"   *47*

   "Dance of the Dead"   *54*

   "Do Not Forsake Me Oh My Darling"   *63*

   "It's Your Funeral"   *68*

   "Checkmate"   *75*

   "Living in Harmony"   *82*

   "A Change of Mind"   *87*

   "Hammer into Anvil"   *92*

   "The Girl Who Was Death"   *98*

   "Once Upon a Time"   *103*

   "Fall Out"   *109*

Chapter Two: NOTES, ANECDOTES, AND NONSENSE   *119*

Chapter Three: THE GREAT DEBATES   *145*

Chapter Four: WHAT DOES IT ALL MEAN?   *163*

Chapter Five: TALKING WITH McGOOHAN   *175*

   Patrick McGoohan Films   *181*

APPENDIX A: Sources of Information   *185*

APPENDIX B: The Shooting Scripts   *189*

ACKNOWLEDGMENTS

There are two names on the cover of this book, but there are many more behind the scenes. The book could not have been "official" without the strong help and assistance from people at ITC, especially Ed Gilbert, Ben Crimmee, and Murray Horowitz. And the book would not have been done without Bob Miller at Warner Books (who really believed in this project) and our literary agent, Susan Urstadt (who made this happen). Other people who helped bring life to our publication include: Bruce Clark, Michael Pollack, Donna McCrohan, Darrell Moore, Tony Lytle, Stefaan Janssen, David Lawrence, and Gordon Tarn (who gave us inspiration and help when we needed it most). And always, heartfelt thanks to Waleed and Malik and to Carol and Liz.

INTRODUCTION

"I suppose that [The Prisoner] is the sort of thing where a thousand people might have a different interpretation of it, which I think is very gratifying. I am glad that's the way it was, because that was the intention."

—Patrick McGoohan

The *Prisoner* is one of those rare television shows that refuses to surrender to the inevitabilities of time. Produced over twenty years ago, this caustic and penetrating allegory is still alive and kicking—perhaps more popular now than when it first aired. There's meaning in this.

In writing this book, we've been concentrating on what *The Prisoner* means: what it's trying to say, what message is concealed in its allegory, what profundities are to be revealed in places like The Village and in characters like Rover and Number Six. But perhaps the more important question is why, after twenty years, does *The Prisoner* continue to fascinate us? Why, indeed, is this book being written now?

It's easy to say that *The Prisoner* was ahead of its time, but that's missing the point. *The Prisoner* was a product of its time, the same time period that produced the Beatles and Timothy Leary and Vietnam. Many of the episodes have been properly interpreted as expressions of contemporary issues, be it the Vietnam War or recreational drug use or alternative life-styles. But few people watch *The Prisoner* for these reasons. People continue to watch and talk about *The Prisoner* because it remains the most unusual, the most provacative, and the most controversial television series ever produced. It dared to probe the boundaries of what a television series could be, and as such, it is unique and deserving of respect.

1

Behind the scenes of THE SCHIZOID MAN.

It is also extraordinarily entertaining. Each episode is fun to watch, and that point is often neglected by those who, like us, feel compelled to interpret the series, to get at its meaning, to solve the unsolvable riddles. But like Shakespeare, Patrick McGoohan was charged with pleasing two audiences: the casual viewers who are quickly bored and his creative muse who demands a strict allegiance to artistic integrity. Although much of what has been written on *The Prisoner* during the past twenty years has tended to be on the scholarly side, there should be no mistaking that McGoohan was a master entertainer: he knew how to attract an audience and how to keep them watching.

The most difficult aspect of writing this book has been to maintain the balance that McGoohan maintained: to confront the issues but not lose sight of the fact that the show itself had humor, intrigue, and mystery. It's especially difficult when the issues themselves are so profound: the

Leo McKern takes a break during the production of FALL OUT.

individual and society; the philosophical nature of freedom; the concentration and abuse of power; the destructive worship of progress. These are not issues that are hidden under the surface of the series. They're up front, blatant, threatening: they're what the show is all about. Like *1984* and *Brave New World*—the two works of art most often compared with *The Prisoner*—this series was designed to make people confront their society and their life-style, to ask the big questions. But—and this is important—those questions were not posed in a philosophical treatise to university professors. The questions were posed instead in a seventeen-episode network television show that aired in prime time to entertain the general viewing public.

Fans of *The Prisoner* are unlike fans of any other television show. Those who have carried the torch for the past twenty years have been uncompromising in their dedication to the series. They have boldly debated the philosophical questions raised by *The Prisoner*, they are quick to identify "Prisoneresque" problems in modern life, and they have faithfully tended the garden—conducting extensive interviews with even the most minor production personnel, laboring over shooting scripts and musical scores and other papers that may reveal a new fact about the show, and taking great pains to provide other fans from around the world with the most minute details about the making of the series. Indeed, these people are not really common fans but scholars, and much of this book benefits from their extensive scholarship.

We have tried, in compiling this book, to explore the mysteries and mine the riches of *The Prisoner*. It's been a lot of fun. But, frankly, there is much in this series that will never be defined, certain questions that will never be answered. That, according to McGoohan, was the intent of the series: to ignite thousands of equally valid interpretations. Those who insist on answers may find that frustrating. Others, like us, find it to be liberating. We find *The Prisoner* to be a dynamic catalyst of ideas, one that steadfastly refuses to knuckle under to quick and glib interpretations. That's why we're still watching it. That's why we're still debating it. And that's why we're writing about it now, some twenty years after its initial release.

There are several mechanical problems that have to be addressed in order to fully understand the complexities of *The Prisoner*. The most frustrating of these is the proper ordering of the episodes. The order of the episodes in the "Episode Guide" is that under which ITC—the production company—introduced the series to the United States in 1968. It is also the order by which the videocassettes are sold in the United States. This is not the same order by which they originally played in the United Kingdom. And we're still trying to figure out in what order the episodes were actually produced. Indeed, one of the most persistent controversies among *Prisoner* devotees is the original intended order; to date, documentation does not give much support to any "official" order. Because of these problems, it is impossible to determine how any one episode builds on the knowledge gleaned from previous episodes (except, perhaps, for the final episode, "Fall Out," which builds on all that has come before).

Another mechanical problem concerns the discrepancies between shooting scripts and the actual productions, and with the various "lost" episodes that are now being discovered and released on videocassette. The scripts that appear in this book are shooting scripts and at times vary dramatically from the actual programs. The reasons they are different can vary from the necessary trimming of a program into a time slot to a creative decision that was made on the set. Although we are quite grateful for the research that has turned up old scripts and new programs, it does cause problems in determining the intent behind *The Prisoner*; certain observations, unfortunately, have to be qualified to account for the various discrepancies.

In the end, *The Prisoner* was never meant to solve anything. It was meant to provoke and to question and to encourage others to probe and question. Although we have tried to resist the temptation to clarify positions and settle arguments, we're sure that some bias is going to come through or some fact will later be contradicted. That's the danger we run, but if the book helps people better understand the parameters of the series, it's a risk worth taking. Be seeing you. . . .

CHAPTER ONE

PRISONER EPISODE GUIDE

Listed in this chapter are detailed synopses and fanciful observations on all seventeen episodes. For purposes of clarity, the role played by Patrick McGoohan is always referred to as "Number Six." At various points in the episodes, this is not quite accurate (at the beginning we don't know who he is, at the end he is simply called "Sir"); this way, at least, you will always know whom we're discussing. It should also be noted that the detailed opening sequence is only described in the first episode, "Arrival" (which contains a few scenes not included in the other episodes with opening sequences). Any important differences in opening sequences for episodes two through seventeen are discussed in the observations for that episode.

"ARRIVAL": EPISODE ONE

Writers: George Markstein and David Tomblin
Script Editor: George Markstein
Producer: David Tomblin
Director: Don Chaffey
Executive Producer: Patrick McGoohan

CAST
Patrick McGoohan (Number Six), Virginia Maskell (The Woman), Guy Doleman (Number Two), Paul Eddington (Cobb), George Baker (the new Number Two), Angelo Muscat (The Butler), Barbara Yu Ling (Taxi Driver), Stephanie Randall (Maid), Jack Allen (Doctor), Fabia Drake (Welfare Worker), Denis Shaw (Shopkeeper), Oliver MacGreevy (Gardener/Electrician), Frederick Piper (Ex-Admiral), Patsy Smart (Waitress), Christopher Benjamin (Labour Exchange Manager), Peter Swanwick (Supervisor), David Garfield (Hospital Attendant), Peter Brace (1st Guardian), Keith Peacock (2nd Guardian).

CREW
Bernard Williams (Production Manager), Brendan J. Stafford (Director of Photography), Jack Shampan (Art Director), Ron Grainer (Musical Theme), Jack Lowin (Camera Operator), Lee Doig (Editor), Robert Monks (2nd Unit Camera), Gino Marotta (Assistant Director), Wilfred Thompson (Sound Editor), John Bramall (Sound Recordist), Bob Dearberg (Music Editor), Rose Tobias-Shaw (Casting Director), Doris Martin (Continuity), Kenneth Bridgeman (Set Dresser), Pat McDermot (Hairdressing), Eddie Knight (Makeup), Masada Wilmot (Wardrobe).

SYNOPSIS
The opening sequence, which will appear in a condensed form in most of the future episodes, is established. Thunder crashes; dark clouds threaten; a sound of jet aircraft is heard; and then there is silence. A car drives toward the viewer on a deserted runway: it is a sporty Lotus 7, driven by a man we will come to know as Number Six. Close-ups of this man reveal a grim expression, his hair blown back by the wind. The camera is placed overhead, and we watch this man dart through narrow London streets. The car eventually disappears into an underground garage. Suddenly we see Number Six walking down a long corridor, obviously angry. He pulls open the doors at the end of the corridor and confronts a bureaucratic older man sitting at a desk. Number Six paces, argues, and

pounds his fist on the desk—each action punctuated by a clap of thunder. Eventually Number Six takes an envelope from his pocket and throws it on the desk. This envelope, we learn, contains his letter of resignation.

The resignation letter is put through bureaucratic channels: a picture of Number Six on a computer card is defaced with the *x*'s from a typewriter. This defaced photo is picked up by the arms of a mechanical robot and deposited in a file cabinet that reads "Resigned." Meanwhile, Number Six has returned in his car to a townhouse and is packing his suitcase furiously. A black hearse pulls up outside the door. A tall man, looking very much like an undertaker, walks slowly to the front door. Gas fumes are pumped in through the keyhole of the house, causing Number Six to stagger and fall. The camera shows a close-up of Number Six, unconscious.

Number Six awakes, is groggy, and moves slowly toward the window for air. He opens the venetian blinds, looks out, and sees not the London streets outside his townhouse, but The Village—a candy-colored storybooklike community. A close-up of Number Six's face expresses shock and confusion.

Off balance and in a state of panic, Number Six runs out of his new dwelling and begins to scout out his location. Nobody is in sight, although Number Six knows that he is being watched. He eventually spots a middle-aged waitress setting tables. From her he learns that the place is called, simply, The Village. He tries to make a phone call and learns that only "local" calls are permitted. A buggylike vehicle marked "taxi" drives up next to him, and the driver offers him a ride. He learns that the taxi provides only "local" service. Number Six goes to a place called "general stores" and asks the shopkeeper for a map; he is provided with only local maps that chart The Village and its boundaries: the mountains and the sea. Number Six returns to his dwelling and observes for the first time the sign that reads "6 private" on his doorway. Once inside, he receives a phone call and is summoned to meet Number Two at The Green Dome.

The conversation with Number Two gets to the heart of the matter, revealing why Number Six has been brought against his will to this strange location: a lot of people (identities never given) are curious about Number Six's resignation. They want to know why he resigned, and they demonstrate a vast knowledge of Number Six's personal and public life. If Number Six cooperates with the investigation—if he tells them why he resigned—he will perhaps be given a position of authority. Number Six has no intention of revealing his motives and delivers the famous lines "I will not make any deals with you. I've resigned. I will not be pushed, filed, stamped, indexed, briefed, debriefed, or numbered. My life is my own." After this meeting, Number Two offers Number Six a

Number Six learns that only local taxi rides are provided in The Village.

helicopter tour of The Village, giving special emphasis to the fact that
The Village has its own graveyard.

After the helicopter tour is complete, Number Six roams the grounds
and observes many curious sites, the most curious being an attack on a
man by a big, menacing, bouncing balloonlike thing. The attack balloon,
which we will come to know as Rover, causes every Villager to freeze
in his or her tracks—everyone except Number Six and the man being
attacked. After witnessing this odd and brutal demonstration of power,
Number Six returns to his dwelling.

An early attempt is made to lure Number Six into betraying his
confidence: a personal maid is assigned to his dwelling, and this maid
sheds a few tears in an attempt to get Number Six to talk. He won't, and
Number Two—watching the interchange from a surveillance device with

the bald-headed Supervisor—admits that Number Six will be a difficult prisoner.

Frustrated, Number Six makes a desperate attempt to escape by jumping in a "taxi" and driving off to the beach. After battling a pair of Guardians there, he is subdued by Rover—the big, white, bouncing weather balloon—and, subsequently, hospitalized. In the hospital Number Six is placed in a bed next to an old friend named Cobb, and the two share thoughts about The Village. They are separated and Number Six overhears a hospital attendant saying that his friend Cobb jumped out a window and killed himself. Number Six, after being released from the hospital, makes his way to The Green Dome to ask some pointed questions about Cobb's death. He finds himself face to face with a new Number Two. This new Number Two provides little information except to inform Number Six that "for official purposes, everyone has a number. Yours is Number Six." On leaving Number Two's office, Number Six replies: "I am not a number; I am a person." He then returns to his dwelling.

Number Six meets a woman at Cobb's funeral and learns later, at a concert, that she and Cobb were planning an escape attempt before the suicide. The woman encourages Number Six to take on Cobb's role in the attempt. The escape, which involves The Village helicopter, is made possible by the woman's possession of a special device called an "electropass." This device, which is worn like a watch, can disengage the alarm system (and thus get Number Six past Rover). Number Six is suspicious of the woman's motives, especially after seeing her in Number Two's office. But, against hope, he trusts her and follows her escape plan to the letter. The electropass does indeed allow him to walk right past Rover into the helicopter. He starts the helicopter and starts flying away toward freedom. Once in the air, however, the helicopter takes on a life of its own and steers Number Six back to The Village. The entire escape plan was obviously engineered by Number Two to teach Number Six an important lesson: escape is not possible. It becomes obvious that Number Two had some help in the execution of his plan. It wasn't the woman, who sincerely believed that Number Six would be able to escape. It was Cobb, who is alive and well and working for "new masters." The friend he thought was dead was working against him all the time.

OBSERVATIONS

- Number Six (McGoohan) is like a caged animal: he paces, he scowls, he loses his temper, he thumps his fist on tables. In short, he's confused, stubborn, and angry. These are qualities that will remain characteristic of Number Six in future episodes, but nowhere are they as primal, as basic, and as raw as they are in this first episode.

• In comparing the character Number Six in *The Prisoner* with his previous role as John Drake in *Secret Agent*, McGoohan has said that both men get in trouble, but that John Drake was always able to bully or think his way out of the situation by the end of the show. Not so for *The Prisoner*, although it appears in "Arrival" that this character, Number Six, is working under old presumptions. Number Six is obviously irritated by his incarceration, but—in this episode, at least—he appears to believe that escape is not only possible but inevitable, and that next week he'll be confronting new villains in a new part of the not-so-free world. That's his first mistake in judgment. It won't be his last.

• It is difficult for the viewer to kick back, relax, and enjoy the show. There is simply too much going on. Within the first ten minutes of "Arrival," we are introduced to a phenomenally different world: one with its own sense of fashion, its own odd vocabulary, its own distinct methods of transportation, housing, communications, and entertainment. It appears to be an idyllic sort of place, a utopia: colorful, lively, peaceful, a place of leisure. But there's a dark underbelly to this com-

Rover waits patiently for Number Six, who has just learned one humbling lesson: escape from The Village is no easy task.

munity: surveillance equipment is placed within the eyes of Greek statuettes that adorn the neatly mown lawns; people address each other not by name but by number; only local telephone calls and taxi rides are permitted; the easy-listening music that is pumped into the individual housing units cannot be turned off; and there's this big white, bouncing, threatening thing that makes loud noises and causes people to run and hide. On his first encounter with another human being, Number Six is told, quite frankly, that he's in The Village, as if that were a sufficient answer to his question: "Where am I?"

- There is little question about why this man we only know as Number Six has been brought to The Village. Number Two—the top authority in the village, the person who makes decisions—is very specific in his first conversation with Number Six: "The information in your head is priceless. I don't think you realize what a valuable property you have become. A man like you is in great demand on the open market. . . . A lot of people are curious about what lies behind your resignation. You've had a brilliant career. They want to know why you suddenly left."

    It is obvious from the start that the authorities of The Village want information. It is equally apparent that Number Six won't talk. But there's a casual quality to this confrontation in "Arrival." Indeed, this entire episode is geared more toward laying the groundwork of the series than with developing plotlines or characters.

- The game of chess is introduced here, in the first episode. It will be played, in various forms, throughout the series. Although many people have found the game of chess to be full of symbolic implications, its most obvious meaning is stated in "Arrival" when the ex-admiral says to the woman who is helping Number Six to escape: "We're all pawns."

- In this episode Number Six seems much more willing to trust people than he does in future episodes. Although he is able to see through the crocodile tears of his personal maid, he is struck by the tears that are shed at a funeral by The Woman (played by Virginia Maskell). This honest display of emotion is enough to convince Number Six that the woman may be trustworthy (although he still has certain doubts, especially when he sees her depart from a meeting with Number Two). And she is trustworthy. But what Number Six doesn't realize is that the woman's emotions are being manipulated in a complex effort to trip him up. And at the end of the episode, we learn that a man he trusted immediately—his old friend Cobb—was quick to betray that trust. This inability to determine whether somebody is trustworthy will be a major factor in the entire series. Indeed, the authorities of The Village play on the paranoid atmosphere, and there are many Villagers who are quite suspicious of Number Six.

- The final credits of this episode do not reveal where *The Prisoner* was shot. It simply says: "Made on location and at Metro-Goldwyn-Mayer Studios, Borehamwood, England." During the original broadcast of the series, the location was a well-kept secret, not revealed until the final episode, when the opening credits identified Portmeirion Resort in Wales as the actual location.

- A sign appears in the background of this episode that reads: "Questions are a burden to others; answers are a prison for oneself." This motto will reappear in various forms throughout the series, and it deftly captures much of the sentiment about *The Prisoner*. Although it is intended to keep The Villagers in line, it is one of the few things within the series that actually addresses the word "prison." Could it be that the true prisoners are those who really believe they have the answers to questions?

The game of chess figures prominently in many episodes of *The Prisoner.*

"THE CHIMES OF BIG BEN": EPISODE TWO

Writer: Vincent Tilsley
Script Editor: George Markstein
Producer: David Tomblin
Director: Don Chaffey
Executive Producer: Patrick McGoohan

CAST

Patrick McGoohan (Number Six), Leo McKern (Number Two), Nadia Gray (Nadia), Finlay Currie (General), Richard Wattis (Fotheringay), Angelo Muscat (The Butler), Kevin Stoney (Colonel J), Christopher Benjamin (Number Two's Assistant), David Arlen (Karel), Peter Swanwick (Supervisor), Hilda Barry (Number 38), Jack Le-White (First Judge), John Maxim (Second Judge), Lucy Griffiths (Third Judge).

CREW

Bernard Williams (Production Manager), Brendan J. Stafford (Director of Photography), Jack Shampan (Art Director), Ron Grainer (Musical Theme), Jack Lowin (Camera Operator), Spencer Reeve (Editor), Robert Monks (2nd Unit Camera), Gino Marotta (Assistant Director), Wilfred Thompson (Sound Editor), John Bramall (Sound Recordist), Bob Dearberg (Music Editor), Rose Tobias Shaw (Casting Director), Doris Martin (Continuity), Kenneth Bridgeman (Set Dresser), Eddie Knight (Makeup), Pat McDermot (Hairdressing), Masada Wilmot (Wardrobe).

SYNOPSIS

The Village is going to sponsor an arts and crafts show, and everyone is invited to participate. Number Six shows no interest in the show but does enjoy a good game of chess with the General. After playing chess and entering into a crafty discussion with Number Two, he notices that a striking young woman is brought to The Village in a helicopter. He soon learns that her name is Nadia, her number is Eight, and she will be living in the quarters next door to Number Six.

Number Six observes this woman first with some amusement and caution. He learns that she is being held in The Village because she resigned, much like Number Six. He learns that her name is Nadia Rakowski, an Estonian. And he learns that she is as distrustful of him as he is of her. When Nadia tries to escape by swimming desperately out into the sea—only to be brutally captured and returned by Rover—Number

Six starts to think that maybe she is exactly who she says she is, and maybe she can be trusted.

After her escape attempt, Nadia is brought to the hospital and interrogated by Number Two. Number Six is invited to watch. The interrogation turns nasty; Nadia tries to kill herself. Number Six, feeling compassion for Nadia, strikes a deal with Number Two to stop the torture. If Nadia is let free, he agrees to cooperate with Number Two by entering the arts and crafts competition. It's an arrangement that amuses Number Two, and one that he agrees to.

Nadia and Number Six quickly become confidants. The two of them begin to trust one another and to share ideas for escape. Number Six decides to build a boat from the lumber in the forest, which will be used in an escape attempt. To conceal the fact that he is building a boat, he tells Number Two that he is entering an abstract wood carving in the arts and crafts competition. Number Two appears quite satisfied with this and enjoys watching Number Six labor over the construction of the boat. Nadia intimates that she knows the location of The Village—that it is on the Baltic Coast, in Lithuania, only thirty miles from the Polish border. With this information, Number Six is confident that a successful escape can be put into action.

The Butler serves coffee as Number Six and Number Two engage in a battle of wits.

Number Two and The Butler share a private moment during the arts-and-crafts competition, in which the favorite artistic subject is . . . Number Two.

Number Six enters three wood pieces into the competition, and he calls his abstract creation "Escape." These three wood pieces will, of course, make up the parts of a sailboat. All the other entries in the competition are various portraitures and sculptures of Number Two. Number Six purchases one of these items—a tapestry of Number Two that will make a nice sail.

Number Six and Nadia sail out into the ocean, with their sites set on Poland. Number Two, through various surveillence techniques, catches them in the act and sends Rover to stop them. Rover does capture the boat, but Number Six and Nadia escape to the land. A contact of Nadia's meets them on shore and agrees to help transport them to London. Number Six's watch has stopped, and he borrows one from Nadia's contact. Nadia's contact hides them in packing cases and books the cases through Danzig to Copenhagen to London. It appears, during the journey, that Nadia is falling in love with Number Six. They arrive, in cases, in Number Six's London office. In London, Number Six and Nadia are met by Colonel J and Fotheringay, two of Number Six's old colleagues. The sounds of London fill the air.

Colonel J is suspicious of Number Six, believing him to have turned double agent on the British government. He wants to know why Number Six resigned, and Number Six agrees to answer that question if Nadia is guaranteed protection. Colonel J agrees to the terms and asks the question. Number Six is about to answer when he hears the final chime of Big Ben. He looks at his watch. The time on his watch, eight o'clock, is the same as the chime from Big Ben. But there is a one-hour difference between Polish time and London time. This calculation is enough to tip off Number Six that something is wrong. Now suspicious, he starts pulling electrical cords out of their sockets. All the London city sounds stop immediately. The silence is deafening. He opens a cabinet to discover a reel-to-reel tape recorder. He plugs the electrical cord back in, the tape recorder starts up, and the London sounds resume. Number Six walks out of the office, down the hallway, and opens a door to the outside. The scene is not London at all but, instead, The Village. Nadia, Fotheringay, and Colonel J were all conspirators in this latest attempt to extract information from Number Six.

OBSERVATIONS

• "The Chimes of Big Ben" is a key episode in the series, one of the original seven as proposed by Patrick McGoohan. It is a thoroughly entertaining episode, a nail-biting suspense piece that provides lots of information on *The Prisoner* and has been fertile ground for much discourse of the series as a whole. Among other things, it marks the first appearance of Leo McKern as Number Two.

- "The Chimes of Big Ben" almost appears out of place as the second episode in the series. Number Six has made what seems to be a radical transformation in character. In the first episode he was angry, inconsolable, and unwilling to conform. In "Chimes," Number Six is a master player of The Village's game: outwardly polite, charming, apparently at ease with himself, if not his situation. Some have used this apparent change of character to argue that "The Chimes of Big Ben" should be scheduled later in the series, although it has been documented that the screenwriter, Vincent Tilsley, believed this to be the second episode when he was given the writing assignment.

- The escape plan devised by Number Six, based on the mistaken knowledge of The Village's location, is wonderfully ingenious, and it offers key insights into the depth of Number Six's talents: this is a man who can build a working boat from felled trees; who understands the intricacies of nautical principles; who is as comfortable discussing abstract art as he is plotting an escape plan. Number Six has the brains, the brawn, and the desire to better his situation. He appears to be a type of superman, but even that won't enable him to beat the system.

- The surprise but inevitable ending makes the viewer rethink what transpired during the show. Nadia was a plant; Number Six's escape was encouraged by The Village to extract information; the location of The Village remains uncertain. However, we know now that two of Number Six's former British superiors are not only aware of his incarceration, but actively involved in it.

- The acronym for "Chimes of Big Ben" is CODB, the name of Number Six's friend who tried to double-cross him in "Arrival."

- The script pokes some fun at abstract art in this episode, as Number Six elaborately explains the meaning of his work. This piece of art, which all the good-intentioned judges are at a loss to explain (but believe in nonetheless), is simply a practical creation that is intended to help the artist escape.

- There are two versions of "The Chimes of Big Ben"—the one that played on television and a recently discovered "alternate version" that was prepared for press screenings before *The Prisoner* first aired. The "alternate version" is revealing in details about the symbols of the show, especially the penny-farthing bicycle. At the very end of the show, after the credits have rolled, the wheels of the penny-farthing start turning, and they become the Earth and the universe. The Earth, spinning on its axis, comes toward the television screen and the word "POP" comes from nowhere to fill the entire screen. This word "POP" will be explained in the episode "Once Upon a Time." Apparently it was designed to be one more mystery and is reinforced during "The Chimes of Big Ben" when, in one scene, the nursery rhyme "Pop Goes the Weasel" can be heard.

There are many other differences between the two versions of "Chimes." The recently discovered version has an entirely different musical theme, composed by Wilfred Josephs. The opening sequence

Kevin Stoney stars as The Colonel, a man who worked with Number Six before he went to The Village, and a man who is most certainly involved in Number Six's incarceration.

is also quite different from that seen in "Arrival" or any other episode with an opening sequence. The most dramatic change within the episode concerns Number Six's use of an astronomical device called a triquetrum, which Number Six calls "a makeshift Greek device for discovering one's whereabouts." The entire use of this instrument was edited out of the final version.

• Vincent Tilsley, who wrote this episode and the original script for "Do Not Forsake Me Oh My Darling" (which was completely rewritten) is now a psychotherapist, practicing in England.

• Once again, Number Six is betrayed by a woman (although the betrayal in the first episode appears to have been unwitting). We are unaware of any scripting directions that call specifically for the untrustworthiness of women in *The Prisoner*, although it is a theme that will surface over and over. It becomes most heated in the eighth episode, "Dance of the Dead."

"A. B. AND C.": EPISODE THREE

Writer: Anthony Skene
Script Editor: George Markstein
Producer: David Tomblin
Director: Pat Jackson
Executive Producer: Patrick McGoohan

CAST
Patrick McGoohan (Number Six), Katherine Kath (Engadine), Sheila Allen (Number Fourteen), Colin Gordon (Number Two), Peter Bowles ("A"), Angelo Muscat (The Butler), Georgina Cookson (Blonde Lady), Annette Carrell ("B"), Lucille Soong (Flower Girl), Bettine Le Beau (Maid at Party), Terry Yorke (Thug), Peter Brayham (Thug), Bill Cummings (Henchman).

CREW
Bernard Williams (Production Manager), Brendan J. Stafford (Director of Photography), Jack Shampan (Art Director), Jack Lowin (Camera Operator), Geoffrey Foot (Editor), Ron Grainer (Musical Theme), Albert Elms (Incidental Music), Gino Marotta (Assistant Director), Peter Elliott (Sound Editor), John Bramall (Sound Recordist), Eric Mival (Music Editor), Rose Tobias-Shaw (Casting Director), Doris Martin (Continuity), Kenneth Bridgeman (Set Dresser), Eddie Knight (Makeup), Pat McDermot (Hairdressing), Masada Wilmot (Wardrobe).

SYNOPSIS
Number Two is anxious, under great stress, and afraid of his superiors. His assignment is to find out why Number Six resigned; if he is unsuccessful, it is apparent that actions will be taken against him. In an early conversation with his superiors, Number Two states: "I know I'm not indispensable." Number Two is desperate and decides to experiment with a new drug application that, as yet, has only been tested on animals. Number Six will be the first human subject.

The drug, developed by Number Fourteen, makes it possible to enter the dreams of the subject and to control, by suggestion, what is going on in the dreams. Furthermore, these dreams can be converted into electronic impulses that are visible as images on a television screen. In other words, the scientists can actually watch the dream play out on a monitor. The subject can undergo only three injections of the drug; the fourth would surely be fatal.

Number Two believes that Number Six would confide his inner secret (why he resigned) to one of three people if he was not incarcerated in The Village. These three people are identified only as "A," "B," and "C," and each drug-induced session is designed to re-create a confrontation between Number Six and one of these three individuals. The theory is that Number Six would, in a prepared dream, tell his innermost secret to one of the three persons.

Number Six is brought unconscious into the laboratory and injected with the experimental drug. His head is wired to various electrodes, and a circular cassette is inserted in the dream machine. This cassette contains a film of Madame Engadine's celebrated parties in Paris. It is a place that "A," "B," and "C"—as well as Number Six—were all known to frequent. The dream begins to take form on the television screen, and Number Six is seen in conversation with Madame Engadine. Knowing that the experiment is going to work, Number Two insists that character "A" be introduced. Again, a cassette is placed in the machine, and character "A" appears.

Number Fourteen and Number Two discuss the latest developments in drug-enduced dream manipulation.

Character "A" is a man who once worked side by side with Number Six; he subsequently turned double agent to work for the enemy. Number Two believes that perhaps Number Six would follow in his colleague's treasonous footsteps. In this dream, however, Number Six reveals nothing to "A" and even treats the former colleague with disdain. Number Two is upset that nothing is revealed in the encounter but eventually concedes that "at least I know it wasn't 'A' he was selling out to." Number Two is anxious to test out "B" in the dreams, but Number Fourteen insists that a twenty-four-hour rest is necessary in between sessions.

During the twenty-four-hour rest period, Number Six notices the needle mark on his wrist, where the drug was injected. He also sees Number Fourteen outside his dwelling and recognizes her as someone from his dreams. Number Six knows that something is going on, and he craftily discusses his observations with Number Two. Although unable to confirm any of his suspicions during the meeting, he makes his presence felt, and Number Two frets and worries. Within twenty-four hours Number Six is again in the laboratory, unconscious.

Number Fourteen and Number Two once again subject Number Six to the drug-induced dream experiment, this time introducing a woman known as "B." This woman, "who even looks like a spy," is an old friend of Number Six's, and the two of them spend most of their time dancing and flirting. In fact, Number Six and "B" are too friendly; they don't address the questions that Number Two wants answered. The drug starts to wear off. Number Fourteen, under great pressure from Number Two, suggests that it might be possible to put words into "B"'s mouth. It's an idea that Number Two likes and puts into action. Suddenly "B" is asking Number Six pertinent questions, such as "Why did you resign?" Furthermore, she insists that if Number Six doesn't cooperate with her, she will be killed by "them." Number Six knows something is up and suspects this woman is an imposter—even in his dream. After getting the wrong answers to some very personal questions ("How old is your son?" "What is your son's name?"), Number Six departs the scene. Number Two, watching anxiously, throws down "B"'s file in disgust.

Number Six awakens the next morning to find two needle marks on his wrist. This time he's determined to find out what's going on. He secretly follows Number Fourteen, who unwittingly leads him to the laboratory. After Number Fourteen leaves the laboratory, Number Six breaks in and looks around. He sees the cassettes, the files on "A," "B," and "C," and starts to make sense of the situation. Finally, he discovers the hypodermic syringe that contains the drug to be used in the next test. Number Six empties out the drug and fills the syringe with water. He returns to his dwelling.

Number Six is brought unconscious, for the third consecutive night, into the laboratory. This time they're going to bring "C" into his dreams, but—this is important—they have no photograph of "C"; they're not quite sure who he (or she) is. Number Six is injected with the drug (which is actually water), and the suggestion of "C" is implanted. At first, to the great surprise of Number Two, it appears that Madame Engadine is "C"—she asks for the secret papers, then promises to introduce Num-

Was Number Six going to sell out to this foreign agent identified by the letter "A"? No way.

ber Six to her superior. Madame Engadine drives Number Six to a mysterious location where he is to meet her superior, who is being called "D" by Number Fourteen. Number Six and "D" meet. This mystery man is wearing a mask. Number Two is incredibly excited about the meeting and believes that the revelation of "D"'s character will save his job, perhaps his life. Number Six refuses to turn over the papers until the mask is stripped from "D"'s face. After a minor struggle, Number Six strips off the mask; underneath the mask is . . . Number Two. Number Six has beaten Number Two at his own game. Number Six then manipulates his dream to act as if he is walking into the laboratory, where Number Two and Number Fourteen are conducting their experiment. Number Six then hands the unrevealed papers to Number Two. Inside the envelope are travel brochures. Number Six then says: "I wasn't selling out. That was not the reason I resigned." The experiment has failed. The phone rings for a very nervous Number Two.

Madame Engadine always threw the best parties.

OBSERVATIONS

- "A. B. and C." explores flaws within the characters of the authorities. Number Two, artfully played by Colin Gordon, is assigned the task of extracting information from Number Six. Number Two is painfully aware that if his attempts are not successful, his job—perhaps his life—is on the line. It's a bureaucratic problem: Number Two must answer to a hierarchical system that has little patience for failure. Number Two understands all too well the tentative nature of his situation and is willing to take extreme measures in the protection of his job. Although we will meet several Number Twos who are "afraid of their masters," this is one of the few who appears willing to risk Number Six's life in order to extract information.

- The drug-oriented experiments performed on Number Six give evidence that The Village represents a society of high-technological feats and standards. It is remarkable that a method has been devised in which the dreams of a human being can be monitored, influenced, and altered. That the society would use these technological innovations to extract information reveals a major conflict within *The Prisoner*: technological standards may increase, but ethical ones do not.

- The stunning victory won by Number Six at the end of "A. B. and C." is his first real victory of the series, and it is revealing of a man whose final motives have been seriously altered by his situation. In the first two episodes Number Six wanted out. In this episode he simply wants to maintain his identity and the information in his head. In doing so he not only survives intact, but he effectively defeats an authoritative individual—Number Two, who must now answer for his failure to break Number Six. A lot can be learned about this series by identifying which victories are won by Number Six and which are lost.

- Number Two drinks a lot of milk in this episode, which leads some to believe that he may have an ulcer. It's certainly in keeping with the character's nervous state of mind.

"FREE FOR ALL": EPISODE FOUR

Writer: Patrick McGoohan
Script Editor: George Markstein
Producer: David Tomblin
Director: Patrick McGoohan
Executive Producer: Patrick McGoohan

CAST

Patrick McGoohan (Number Six), Eric Portman (Number Two), Rachel Herbert (Number Fifty-eight), George Benson (Labour Exchange Manager), Angelo Muscat (The Butler), Harold Berens (Reporter), John Cazabon (Man in Cave), Dene Cooper (Photographer), Kenneth Benda (Supervisor), Holly Doone (Waitress), Peter Brace (1st Mechanic), Alf Joint (2nd Mechanic).

CREW

Bernard Williams (Production Manager), Brendan J. Stafford (Director of Photography), Jack Shampan (Art Director), Jack Lowin (Camera Operator), Geoffrey Foot (Editor), Ron Grainer (Musical Theme), Albert Elms (Incidental Music), Robert Monks (2nd Unit Cameraman), Gino Marotta (Assistant Director), Wilfred Thompson (Sound Editor), John Bramall (Sound Recordist), Eric Mival (Music Editor), Rose Tobias-Shaw (Casting Director), Doris Martin (Continuity), Kenneth Bridgeman (Set Dresser), Eddie Knight (Makeup), Pat McDermot (Hairdressing), Masada Wilmot (Wardrobe).

SYNOPSIS

The reigning Number Two suggests that Number Six become a candidate for the office of Number Two. Immediately suspicious, Number Six asks a few pointed questions about the democratic procedures of The Village. He doesn't receive satisfactory answers, but he is told that, if elected, Number One "will no longer be a mystery to you."

Number Six doesn't accept or reject this invitation to be a candidate, but he makes a spontaneous speech to The Villagers, who have assembled outside and are responding to the cue cards held up by The Butler. Number Six proclaims to the populace that he intends "to discover who are the prisoners, and who the warders." Number Two himself applauds the renegade speech. Immediately following the speech, placards carrying Number Six's picture are carried around by joyous Villagers who are obviously enjoying the ceremony of a hard-fought campaign. Reporters from The Village newspaper, *The Tally Ho*, ask questions of this new candidate and print fabricated answers. Number Six is annoyed at the apparent disregard for his real message, and he is somewhat taken aback by the speed at which Villagers are warming to his candidacy. It appears that, whether he has accepted it or not, he's in the heat of the campaign.

A woman speaking an unidentified foreign language is assigned to Number Six as a driver and as a sort of personal assistant for the duration of the campaign. The woman, Number Fifty-eight, is downright strange: her great enthusiasm is oddly exaggerated, and she insists on following Number Six wherever he goes. Number Six is somewhat irritated by his inability to communicate with Number Fifty-eight, but his energies are spent primarily on this new campaign.

Number Six hits the campaign trail and finds unexpected, enthusiastic support from the Villagers.

In his first act of defiance, Number Six challenges the robotlike councilmen who have assembled with Number Two in the Town Hall. He asks too many questions—penetrating questions, such as "To what race or country do you owe allegiance?" "Whom do you represent?" "Who elected you?" "Whose side are you on?" Number Two is distressed by this serious "breach of etiquette." To make Number Six an acceptable candidate, he is put through a series of brainwashing exercises. After the brainwashing, Number Six hits the campaign trail with the zeal of a true performer: promising everything, saying nothing. The crowd goes wild.

After campaigning mindlessly, Number Six relaxes with his personal assistant, Number Fifty-eight. At one point in their conversation, after it appears that they are communicating, Number Six becomes frightened and initiates a mad and desperate escape attempt. He takes to the sea in a speedboat and is captured and returned by Rover. He is brought to the hospital, brainwashed once again, and released to make more meaningless speeches (at one time promising fall, winter, summer, and spring; at another, in a debate with Number Two, promising less work . . . and more play).

Just before the election, Number Six is led by Number Fifty-eight to an underground therapy zone, where one can drink alcoholic beverages in privacy. There he encounters Number Two, who appears to have drunk to excess. The beverage served Number Six, however, had been spiked with something. Number Two had been in on the spiking all along and appears satisfied with the result.

On election day Number Six wins easily, making him the new Number Two. He assumes the office at The Green Dome and starts to play with various electronic devices in Number Two's quarters. Number Fifty-eight also starts toying around with the devices, and then, suddenly, she takes on the characteristics of a radically different person. No longer is she the overzealous assistant. Now she is a grim, powerful manipulator. She subjects Number Six to one more hypnotic, brainwashing maneuver and then—saying, "Tic, tic"—starts slapping Number Six across the face. Number Six, suddenly awakened by this, grabs the public-address telephone and tells everyone in The Village to flee, saying, "I will immobilize all electronic controls. You are free to go." Number Six himself attempts to flee. He makes a mad dash out of the office and winds up in a strange underground room, in which a group of Rover worshipers sit silently around the balloonlike Rover, wearing dark glasses. Number Six is cornered by a few thugs and beaten badly. He is then carried back to the office at The Green Dome, where Number Fifty-eight—now wearing the badge of Number Two—awaits him.

This woman now speaks perfect English. She makes it very clear that Number Six fell victim to a trap that was set in motion long ago, and she sternly asks: "Will you never learn?... Are you ready to talk?" Dumbfounded, Number Six is removed from the offices of Number Two and returned to his original quarters. The man we once thought was

Number Six's combative tendencies can be temporarily eliminated through simple brainwashing techniques.

Number Two is now flying away in a helicopter. The woman we once thought was Number Fifty-eight is in control as Number Two. In a transmission between the helicopter and The Green Dome, the female Number Two says good-bye to the man and signs off with: "Give my regards to the homeland."

OBSERVATIONS

• This episode, written and directed by Patrick McGoohan, is one of his proclaimed favorites; and, indeed, it is one of the favorites of *Prisoner*

There are times when Number Six would prefer to drive the taxi himself.

fans everywhere. It's an assertively cerebral exercise—a political morality play that boldly takes on democratic candidates and systems. Candidates make meaningless promises. Newspapers print only what they want to print. The electorate is more interested in the ceremony than in the issues. There is very little here that is subtle or understated. The viewer gets the point, and the only surprise is that this type of thing played as entertainment on television.

• When this episode was first broadcast in Great Britain, the violent scene near the end—in which Number Six is badly beaten while odd-looking Rover worshipers look on—was not aired; it was considered too violent. The scene is now included in most broadcasts and is on the videocassettes. It is a remarkable scene, primarily because of this strange Rover cult. In no other episode will Villagers interact with Rover in such a mysterious way. The ritual is never explained.

• It is curious that alcoholic beverages are not allowed in The Village (all that is served at the Cat and Mouse nightclub are nonalcoholic beverages that taste alcoholic). Could it be that Villagers are more apt to rebel and question if they indulge in drink?

• Number Six is flat-out defeated at the end of this episode. He has gained nothing. He is made vulnerable to the authorities because he entertains the idea of gaining power (being elected Number Two). Much of this episode, then, can be seen as the study of a candidate's motivations. Although his motivations are suspect once he has been brainwashed, he does enter the race with a clear mind. Some observers have noted that Number Six's ego trips him up—that his desire for power is some type of character flaw subject to exploitation. But there's probably something more political going on here. Number Six's flaw is more likely the belief (however tentative) that the possibility exists for change within the system. The system, as portrayed here, is inflexible, manipulative, and—no matter how many elections they run   totalitarian. There is no room for change.

It should be noted that there is no clear evidence that Number Six actually decided to run for office; he was just caught up in the clamor. Some people believe Number Six had no sights on the office of Number Two; he simply wanted to take advantage of an opportunity to make his thoughts known to The Villagers: to shake them up. Indeed, many people believe that it would be violently out of character for Number Six to actually run for office.

• The press is bashed ruthlessly in this episode, leading some to question McGoohan's personal view of the fourth estate. In a key scene McGoohan refuses to answer the reporters' questions, saying only "No comment." The reporters write their own answers to the questions, with little regard for truth or accuracy. When the newspaper is issued, Number Six's "views" are printed in detail. Next to the article is a photograph of Number Six. Note that the photo is not of Number Six as he appears in The Village. It is a publicity photo of McGoohan himself—the same one that is typed over in the opening sequence.

• The most obvious message of this episode concerns the nature of free elections. The electorate does not elect candidates. They are programmed to vote a certain way. They too are brainwashed, like Number Six. This episode speaks to the idea that a democracy in name only is a sham democracy. It warns that the process of voting does not ensure political freedom (or, as the anarchists would say: "Don't vote, it only encourages them").

• Patrick McGoohan wrote this episode under the pseudonym Paddy Fitz, which is derived from his mother's maiden name, Fitzpatrick.

"SCHIZOID MAN": EPISODE FIVE

Writer: Terence Feely
Script Editor: George Markstein
Producer: David Tomblin
Director: Pat Jackson
Executive Producer: Patrick McGoohan

CAST
Patrick McGoohan (Number Six), Jane Merrow (Alison), Anton Rodgers (Number Two), Angelo Muscat (The Butler), Earl Cameron (Supervisor), Gay Cameron (Number Thirty-six), David Nettheim (Doctor), Pat Keen (Nurse), Gerry Crampton (1st Guardian), Dinney Powell (2nd Guardian).

CREW
Bernard Williams (Production Manager), Brendan J. Stafford (Director of Photography), Jack Shampan (Art Director), Jack Lowin (Camera Operator), Geoffrey Foot (Editor), Ron Grainer (Musical Theme), Albert Elms (Musical Director), Gino Marotta (Assistant Director), Stanley Smith (Sound Editor), John Bramall (Sound Recordist), Eric Mival (Music Editor), Rose Tobias-Shaw (Casting Director), Doris Martin (Continuity), Kenneth Bridgeman (Set Dresser), Eddie Knight (Makeup), Pat McDermot (Hairdressing), Masada Wilmot (Wardrobe).

SYNOPSIS
Number Six helps a woman named Alison (Number Twenty-four) prepare for a mind-reading contest. He looks at special cards (each displaying a shape such as a square or a cross or three wavy lines), thinks about them, and records her "guesses." The woman guesses right 73 percent of the time. She is gifted and furthermore believes that she is telepathically linked to Number Six. At the end of the game Alison clumsily knocks over a bottle while taking a Polaroid snapshot of Number Six. The bottle lands on Number Six's index finger, leaving a bruise at the base of his fingernail. She apologizes and takes a few more snapshots.

That night, something strange happens to Number Six. While sleeping, he is drugged and subjected to an experiment of sorts, in which men push an electrical rod at him and keep encouraging him to use his left hand. When Number Six finally awakens, he is totally confused. The room is not his. The toiletries and the furniture and all other decorative elements have been changed. He looks in the mirror and is alarmed by the fact that he now sports a real mustache and a new hair color (black). He opens the closet and looks inside. His coat is adorned with The Village badge reading "Number Twelve." He gets a phone call from Number Two, who addresses him as Number Twelve and asks him to report to The Green Dome. Number Six leaves his dwelling, walking toward Number Two's office. On the way he is addressed by Villagers as Number Twelve.

When Number Six appears in the offices of Number Two, everybody addresses him as Number Twelve. Furthermore, he is asked to conspire in a plot against . . . himself! The plot is obvious and talked about frankly: a man looking just like Number Six has been employed to act like Number Six. This man (who will be referred to throughout this synopsis as "The Double") has a job, which is to convince Number Six that he is not who he thinks he is. It is believed that if Number Six begins to question his identity, he'll crack.

Number Six strikes a pose for budding photographer/mindreader Number Twenty-four.

Number Six meets The Double, and the two of them engage in various duels, some physical (fencing, shooting), some cerebral (quoting lines of Shakespeare). Number Six is at an obvious physical disadvantage, because he has been programmed to use his left hand instead of his right. He is mentally alert, however, and determined to put this farce to an end. Eventually Number Six suggests that Alison (the mind reader) be used to determine who is the real Number Six and who the fake.

Alison is summoned to the offices and does her mind-reading bit. However, she is better able to read the mind of The Double than she is of Number Six. She further confounds the problem by remembering a

One of these men is the original and the other, "the economy pack."

mole on Number Six's wrist. The Double has such a mole; Number Six does not. Indeed, the real Number Six is visibly shaken, and it appears that the identity-confusion plot is working.

After a restless night, Number Six awakens and suddenly notices the bruise on his fingernail: it has traveled from the base of the fingernail to roughly halfway up. Something isn't right. Obviously some time has been unaccounted for: fingernail bruises do not move up within a day. Number Six looks in the mirror and begins to remember a series of experiments that went on for a matter of days and possibly weeks. He was changed from a righty to a lefty. He was forced to favor flapjacks for breakfast. His beard grew out. His hair was dyed. The most important change was that which made him left-handed, for that impaired him physically. In short, he has been conditioned to act and feel like a different person. To reverse the procedure, he reconditions himself by administering electrical shocks to his hand until he becomes right-handed again.

Number Six finds The Double and confronts him. Fully in charge, with little doubt as to his identity, Number Six forces The Double to reveal information, such as the real password ("Schizoid Man") and The Double's real name (Curtis). With this information, Number Six is prepared to turn the tables on the authorities.

Number Two suspects that something is wrong and sends Rover to the rescue. When Rover finds Number Six, however, he is with The Double—and Rover is unable to tell which one is which. Rover is further confused when both The Double and Number Six give the right password, "Schizoid Man." The Double makes a mistake, however. He tries to run away from Rover. Rover believes this to mean that The Double is Number Six and proceeds to capture and kill him.

Recognizing a chance for real escape, Number Six now starts to impersonate The Double. He telephones Number Two, says that Rover killed Number Six, and then makes plans to be helicoptered out of The Village. Number Six is on dangerous ground and tries to engage in as little conversation as possible. Number Two eventually becomes suspicious but does not have enough evidence to keep his colleague from returning home. Before Number Six leaves, Number Two makes the request, "Give my regards to Susan." Number Six says he will, flies off, and then is returned to The Village. When he exits the helicopter, Number Two says: "Susan died a year ago, Number Six."

OBSERVATIONS

- This episode is an attack on the science of behaviorism, which is especially interesting considering the popularity of B. F. Skinner's writings during the late 1960s, when this series was produced. In many ways the entire *Prisoner* series can be seen as a revolt against the conclusions of behaviorism, especially those outlined in such popular literature as

Walden Two. While both Skinner and McGoohan would agree that freedom is a myth, they would disagree violently about the society's right to influence or control its members for the common good. Skinner's high-principled hero in *Walden Two*, T. E. Frazier, lectures that "we not only *can* control human behavior, we *must*." McGoohan's hero, Number Six, would answer: "The trouble with science is that it can be perverted."

* In this episode we learn that Rover is not infallible. Unable to distinguish between Number Six and The Double (or, as Number Six says, "the original and the economy pack"), Rover mistakingly kills The Double, allowing Number Six to impersonate the impersonator and attempt an escape. This is also the only episode in which Rover is identified by name (after Rover has killed The Double, Number Six calls Number Two and says, "Rover got him").

* While Number Six does attempt to escape at the end of this episode, it is important to note that the focus of the episode is not on escape, but on survival as an individual. Number Six is charged with maintaining his identity, and this he does, victoriously. The boundaries of the struggle have changed. Escape is no longer the main issue; focus is on the maintenance of dignity and self.

* Although never developed, this episode plays with the idea of ESP—a woman named Alison is able to identify the various shapes on cards that Number Six chooses randomly from a pack. Number Six believes more in this very human ability than he does in machines (when trying to prove his identity, he would rather have his mind read than his fingerprints compared by a machine).

* Number Six is tripped up by a method that he himself used to trip up adversaries in "A. B. and C." In this episode he is found out because he didn't know that Curtis's wife had died a year ago. It is personal data that unmasks his imposture. In "A. B. and C.," Number Six trips up the authorities when they impersonate one of Number Six's friends. Number Six asks, "What is your son's name?" It is a question they can't answer, and one that reveals the hoax.

* There is some question as to exactly how long Number Six was subjected to various behavioral experiments. We know that he was there long enough to grow a beard and for the bruise to grow out on his fingernail. In the original shooting script, the duration was to be a full month, documented by calendars reading from February 10 to March 10. In the final version, however, we never know when the procedure ended (although we do know that it started on February 10). The point is important to those who want to figure out the proper ordering of

Number Twenty-four believes that she is telepathically linked with
Number Six.

the episodes. And indeed, the final date may be ambiguous because it conflicts with other dates in future episodes.

• Number Six's impersonation of The Double fails a short time before the dramatic confrontation at the helicopter. While riding in the car toward the helicopter, Number Two makes the statement that Susan had told him a month ago that "you were genuinely quite unflappable." Number Six doesn't react, saying simply, "The job changes us." Number Two, of course, knows that Susan died a year ago, and Number Six has not picked up on this crucial detail.

"THE GENERAL": EPISODE SIX

Writer: Joshua Adam
Script Editor: George Markstein
Producer: David Tomblin
Director: Peter Graham Scott
Executive Producer: Patrick McGoohan

CAST
Patrick McGoohan (Number Six), Colin Gordon (Number Two), John Castle (Number Twelve), Betty McDowall (Professor's Wife), Peter Swanwick (Supervisor), Conrad Phillips (Doctor), Michael Miller (Man in Buggy), Keith Pyott (Waiter), Ian Fleming (Man at Cafe and First Top Hat), Normal Mitchell (Mechanic), Peter Bourne (Projection Operator), George Leech (First Corridor Guard), Jackie Cooper (Second Corridor Guard).

CREW
Bernard Williams (Production Manager), Brendan J. Stafford (Director of Photography), Jack Shampan (Art Director), Jack Lowin (Camera Operator), John S. Smith (Editor), Ron Grainer (Musical Theme), Albert Elms (Incidental Music), Gino Marotta (Assistant Director), Ken Rolls (Sound Editor), John Bramall (Sound Recordist), Eric Mival (Music Editor), Rose Tobias-Shaw (Casting Director), Doris Martin (Continuity), Kenneth Bridgeman (Set Dresser), Eddie Knight (Makeup), Pat McDermot (Hairdressing), Masada Wilmot (Wardrobe).

SYNOPSIS
While sipping coffee in the cafe, Number Six hears what everybody hears on a loudspeaker: students of the three-part history course should return to their dwellings immediately; The Professor is about to give his lecture. Upon this announcement, most of the people leave the cafe. Number Six orders another coffee but is told the cafe is about to close. He begins to engage in a conversation with Number Twelve, who is one of the few people remaining. Number Twelve seems like a nice guy, and the two talk about the three-part course that is to be taught in three minutes. They also observe helicopters overhead, in pursuit of a man. Number Twelve suggests that it's probably The Professor they're after. Number Twelve then leaves; Number Six checks out the action with The Professor.

Indeed, the helicopters are chasing an old man who is desperately crawling along the beach. On the beach Number Six finds a small tape recorder and starts to play it. It is The Professor speaking, about to give some type of warning. Number Six stops the player, buries it in the sand, and is then confronted by various guards. A buggy pulls up, and Number Six is escorted off the beach, dropped off at his dwelling, and encouraged to listen to the lecture.

Number Six does watch the television screen, and The Professor

The Professor's wife says that she is very happy in The Village, but Number Six can't believe her.

eventually appears (after a time-killing introduction by his wife) and tells of the wonders of "speed learn." Today's fifteen-second course is entitled "Europe Since Napoleon." Number Six keeps watching and is strangely hypnotized for fifteen seconds. To his own amazement, he now knows —by rote—such facts as the date of the Treaty of Adrianople and who was Bismarck's ally against the Danish Prince Christian of Glucksburg.

That night Number Six ventures out to the beach to locate the tape recorder. Number Twelve is there with the recorder. Number Six regards him with suspicion, but Number Twelve tries to demonstrate his trustworthiness by handing over the tape recorder. Number Six listens to the message from The Professor, which warns against this speed-learning process and demands that The General be killed. Indeed, The Professor says: "If you wish to be free, there is only one way. Destroy The General."

Number Six starts to scout around The Village, to figure out the mysteries behind The General and The Professor's warning. He eventually stumbles into the room of The Professor's wife and sees that she has created sculptures of various personalities in The Village, including Number Six himself. She appears nervous and refuses to answer any of his questions—except to say that she's an artist and that she and her husband came willingly to The Village. It is obvious, after this discussion, that The Professor is under a good deal of pressure, and his wife is aware of it.

At night Number Twelve visits the dwelling of Number Six, and the two of them conspire to broadcast the subversive message of The Professor. Number Twelve hands Number Six a special token that will enable Number Six to enter the control room, where the messages are broadcast. The plan is put into action. Number Six is able to infiltrate the control room and make his way to the projection room, where the message is actually delivered. After a fight, he assumes the role of projectionist and prepares to project the subversive message. Number Two realizes that Number Six has taken over the projectionist's role. At the very second that the subversive message is to play, Number Six is beaten unconscious and removed from his position. The official message, not the subversive message, is projected.

Afterward, Number Six is interrogated by his co-conspirator Number Twelve, who is demanding—in front of Number Two—to know the identity of those involved in the plan to project a subversive message. Number Six refuses to answer the questions. Number Two, frustrated with the interrogation, decides to have The General answer the questions. The General is revealed as a sophisticated computer, the product of The Professor's hard work. Number Two has total faith in The General's ability to answer any question, even the one most in need of an answer: who helped Number Six infiltrate the control room? Number Two starts feeding The General information and then is about to ask the question when

Number Six intercedes. Number Six proposes that The General be asked a question that can't be answered. Number Two agrees to the challenge, to show The General's infallibility. Number Six types four letters on a sheet of paper and feeds it into The General, which then self-destructs. When asked what the question was that destroyed The General, Number Six responds: "It's insoluble . . . for man or machine. . . . W-H-Y QUESTION MARK. Why?"

OBSERVATIONS

- Number Six found a true conspirator in this episode—Number Twelve. The two of them joined ranks not to escape, but to prevent The Villagers from being brainwashed and manipulated. Number Twelve is one of the few heroes within The Village—a man in authority who is willing to put his career and possibly his life on the line for a noble cause.

- The Professor is a tragic figure, a man with a conscience and genius who is manipulated ruthlessly by the authorities. It again shows McGoohan's great respect and sympathy for men of science and his scorn for the manipulation and perversion of that science. This is a

Number Two proudly displays "The General" to a wounded Number Six.

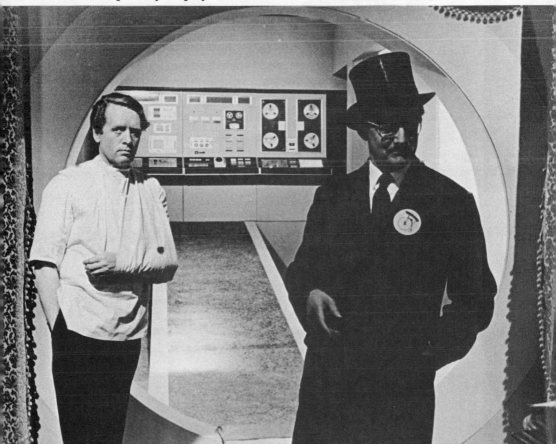

constant theme within *The Prisoner* and is best realized in a future
episode, "Do Not Forsake Me Oh My Darling."

• It is never clear in this episode exactly what the authorities plan to do
with the speed learning. We know that they are creating sculptures of
various people within The Village, and perhaps they are going to replace
the real people with pods, à la *Invasion of the Body Snatchers*. Such
fanciful speculation is probably unimportant, for the real message here
concerns the nature of education in society. People are taught many
facts, but they are not taught to think (to ask "Why?").

• This is the second episode to feature Colin Gordon as the milk-drinking
Number Two; he also appeared in "A. B. and C." It's a difficult reju-
venation, for we were led to believe that Number Two would be se-
verely reprimanded—if not killed—after his failure to get information
in "A. B. and C." This episode, "The General," was actually filmed before
"A. B. and C."—which may explain the inconsistencies in character.
It's another example of the difficulties in determining the proper sequence of episodes.

• We get a first look at the strange corridors that have been built underneath The Village, and we also get a good sense of how rigorously
these corridors of power are protected. We'll see them again in the
final episodes, "Once Upon a Time" and "Fall Out."

• The monstrous computer known to us as The General is quite a scream,
and McGoohan himself has stated that today such a computer would
probably fit in a briefcase. It is one of the few props that actually dates
the series.

• This episode also takes a few moments to poke fun at some contemporary concepts—this time, creative expression. A man who rips pages
out of a book is "creating a fresh concept"; a woman who stands on
her head is "developing a new perspective."

• Number Six demonstrates some artistic skills, even if what he creates
is a very traditional portrait of The Professor's wife (dressed like a
general).

• The speed-learning techniques are broadcast over a television set, and
near the end of this episode we see inside what is basically a television
studio—with sound studios, lecture studios, cameras, and projection
booths. This is not an isolated incident. Throughout the series,
television—whether it is used for entertainment, educational, or surveillance purposes—is portrayed as another scientific advance that has
run amuck. But in the right hands, perhaps . . .

"MANY HAPPY RETURNS": EPISODE SEVEN

Writer: Anthony Skene
Script Editor: George Markstein
Producer: David Tomblin
Director: Joseph Serf
Executive Producer: Patrick McGoohan

CAST
Patrick McGoohan (Number Six), Donald Sinden (The Colonel), Patrick Cargill (Thorpe), Georgina Cookson (Mrs. Butterworth), Brian Worth (Group Captain), Richard Caldicot (Commander), Dennis Chinnery (Gunther), Jon Laurimore (Ernst), Nike Arrighi (Gypsy Girl), Grace Arnold (Maid), Larry Taylor (Gypsy Man).

CREW
Bernard Williams (Production Manager), Brendan J. Stafford (Director of Photography), Jack Shampan (Art Director), Jack Lowin (Camera Operator), Geoffrey Foot (Editor), Ron Grainer (Theme Music), Albert Elms (Musical Director), Robert Monks (2nd Unit Camera), Ernie Morris (Assistant Director), Wilfred Thompson (Sound Editor), John Bramall (Sound Recordist), Eric Mival (Music Editor), Rose Tobias-Shaw (Casting Director), Josie Fulford (Continuity), Kenneth Bridgeman (Set Dresser), Eddie Knight (Makeup), Pat McDermot (Hairdressing), Masada Wilmot (Wardrobe).

SYNOPSIS
Number Six wakes up groggily. He goes to turn on the shower, but no water comes out. He notices that no music is coming in on the loud-speaker. He goes outside to find The Village empty—no people. The umbrellas over the tables are closed. The shops are locked tight. He goes to Number Two's office and is able to enter, but there's no Number Two. He gets in one of the buggies and starts driving around The Village. Everything is confirming his thoughts: The Village has been vacated.

Thinking that maybe an opportunity is brewing, Number Six builds himself a raft. Once the raft is built, he goes into the general store and loads up with various provisions, mostly food and drink. He picks up a camera, goes outside, and takes numerous shots of the unpopulated streets and shops. After the shots are taken, he secures the provisions, sets the raft in the water, and is about to take off when he hears a sound

47

Something isn't quite right in The Village, and Number Six is bound and determined to take advantage of that.

behind him. Almost afraid to look back, Number Six slowly turns and sees only the black cat. Number Six seems to be free.

At sea he jury-rigs a compass to set sail in a known direction. He keeps a journal, day by day. He shaves. After being at sea for weeks, he tires and lies down, apparently unconscious, waiting for the end.

A large boat spots Number Six's raft. The occupants of the boat take

Number Six has been at sea too long.

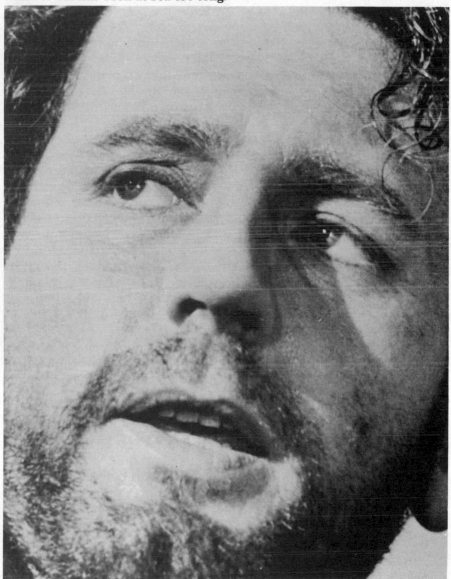

what supplies remain on the raft and then dump Number Six in the ocean, as good as dead. Number Six uses all his strength to pull himself up on the boat, then hatches an ingenious plan to take control of the vessel. Once in command, he sets the boat in direction of a light that is beaming on land. Just before he gets to the light, the boat owners, who we have discovered are actually gunrunners, escape their chains and attack Number Six. Number Six jumps overboard and swims to land.

After a difficult conversation with strange-speaking gypsies, Number Six is shown a road. He wangles a ride on the back of a truck and is deposited in the city of London. Eventually he makes his way to his London home. Mrs. Butterworth, the present occupant of the house, invites him inside.

After a somewhat cautious introduction, the two of them—Number Six and Mrs. Butterworth—become quite friendly. She feeds him finger sandwiches, insists that he shower and shave, and generously answers any question put to her. She even gives him the keys to his Lotus 7 and sees him off at the car. Mrs. Butterworth encourages Number Six (who has given his name as Peter Smith) to return and suggests that she might even bake a cake for his birthday, which is tomorrow. Number Six promises to return and makes his way to his old office to meet his superiors.

Number Six discusses his escape with an old superior known as The Colonel. He shows them the pictures from The Village and tells his incredible tale. But the tale is too incredible. The Colonel and his confidants are suspicious of Number Six, thinking he may be a double agent. After checking his incredible story, detail for detail, they are tentatively willing to believe him. Through a series of calculations, based on Number Six's account of the journey, they determine that The Village must be west of Morocco and southwest of Portugal and Spain. Number Six insists on joining a search party to locate The Village by air.

The search party consists of Number Six and an airplane pilot. They spend hours in the air, searching for The Village. Eventually Number Six sees it and points it out to the pilot. The pilot remains silent, but then suddenly says, "Be seeing you," and ejects Number Six from his seat, leaving him to parachute into The Village. Number Six lands. The Village is as it was when he left it: deserted. He makes his way back to his dwelling. All of a sudden the water in the showers comes on, the coffeepot starts percolating, and the black cat appears in his doorway. Number Six looks at the cat and then looks up at the woman behind it. It is Mrs. Butterworth, holding a birthday cake. She is wearing the badge of Number Two and greets Number Six with the words "Many happy returns."

OBSERVATIONS

• Number Six built a boat from scratch in "The Chimes of Big Ben," and here he builds a raft. We learn much in this episode of Number Six's

It isn't until the very end of the show that Mrs. Butterworth is identified as Number Two.

basic survival and technological skills. At sea he constructs his own compass to set himself on course. When in London, we learn that he had once built a car with his own hands. There is a superman aspect to Number Six that becomes more and more apparent with every episode. He is not superhuman, but he has fully developed the intellectual and physical skills at his disposal.

- The identity of Number Two is concealed during the opening sequence of this episode—a fact that is necessary considering the plot twist at the end of the show, in which Mrs. Butterworth is revealed as Number Two. Still, the voice at the opening of "Many Happy Returns" is male.

- There are two bad luck symbols in this show—a black cat (which also appears in "Dance of the Dead") and a broken plate. It isn't quite clear what's to be made of these symbols, except for the fact that there are unexplained aspects to the world of *The Prisoner* and the world at large.

- The allegory takes full force when Number Six appears in England and is surrounded by symbols of imprisonment such as barbed wire on fences and bars on the windows of a moving truck.

- The location of The Village appears to be solidly identified in this episode. With information provided by Number Six during his journey at sea, the location is plotted west of Morocco and southwest of Portugal and Spain. There is still some life left to the debate over the location of The Village, although most *Prisoner* followers agree that this is indeed the physical location of The Village.

- Number Six is at sea for twenty-five days. He arrives in London on March 18. His birthday is said to be March 19, which, as observed in "Arrival," is McGoohan's own birthday.

- The man who appears at the desk, whom Number Six confronts after leaving Mrs. Butterworth's, is played by George Markstein, the script editor.

- In "The Chimes of Big Ben" we learn at the end that Number Six's British superiors were working for The Village—or at least they were a part of whatever system had incarcerated him. In "Many Happy Returns," we're not so sure. These British superiors appear authentic, and they seem to be honestly concerned about what has happened to Number Six. Casual viewers may think that the pilot of the airplane— the man who ejects Number Six from the plane and back into The Village—was working for the British. But a closer viewing reveals that the airplane pilot first appears in the episode as a milkman (driving a truck that bears a sign reading Pinta Man Is Strong). It is plausible that this milkman, who was working for The Village, overcame the real pilot, took his clothing, and flew Number Six to The Village.

That is exactly what happened in the original script. In fact, in the original script we are introduced to the character who is going to fly the aircraft, and we are privy to a scene in which the milkman and this pilot confront each other. If this had been completed according to the original script, we would have no doubt that the actual airplane pilot was different from the intended airplane pilot. Why would the change have been made in the final version? Perhaps the script was going long, and certain scenes had to be trimmed. More likely, however—considering the importance of this detail—it was decided to leave the situation ambiguous. Although it is fairly clear that the British superiors weren't in on it this time, we can't be certain.

- Mrs. Butterworth, who is identified at the end of this episode as Number Two, wears a black badge with a reversed-out white penny-farthing symbol. This is the only Number Two in the entire series to sport a black badge. No reason is ever given.

- Number Six identifies himself in this episode as Peter Smith. There is no reason to believe that this is his real name.

"DANCE OF THE DEAD": EPISODE EIGHT

Writer: Anthony Skene
Script Editor: George Markstein
Producer: David Tomblin
Director: Don Chaffey
Executive Producer: Patrick McGoohan

CAST

Patrick McGoohan (Number Six), Mary Morris (Number Two), Duncan MacRae (Doctor), Norma West (The Observer), Angelo Muscat (The Butler), Aubrey Morris (Town Crier), Bee Duffell (Psychiatrist), Camilla Hasse (Day Supervisor), Alan White (Dutton), Michael Nightingale (Night Supervisor), Patsy Smart (Night Maid), Denise Buckley (Maid), George Merritt (Postman), John Frawley (Flower Man), Lucy Griffiths (Lady in Corridor), William Lyon Brown (2nd Doctor).

CREW

Bernard Williams (Production Manager), Brendan J. Stafford (Director of Photography), Jack Shampan (Art Director), Jack Lowin (Camera Operator), John S. Smith (Editor), Ron Grainer (Musical Theme), Albert Elms (Musical Director), Robert Monks (2nd Unit Cameraman), Gino Marotta (Assistant Director), Stanley Smith (Sound Editor), John Bramall (Sound Recordist), Eric Mival (Music Editor), Rose Tobias-Shaw (Casting Director), Doris Martin (Continuity), Kenneth Bridgeman (Set Dresser), Eddie Knight (Makeup), Pat McDermot (Hairdressing), Masada Wilmot (Wardrobe).

SYNOPSIS

Number Six is being tortured by an overenthusiastic Doctor. The Doctor has wired electrodes to his head and is interrogating him ruthlessly. The Doctor's assistant, who watches the torture with The Doctor on a monitor, fears for the life of Number Six. When it appears that the interrogation is working, The Doctor hands the telephone to a man named Dutton, who is a former associate of Number Six. Dutton is in a bad state, probably the victim of much experimentation himself. When Number Six refuses to answer Dutton's questions, The Doctor prepares to continue the torture. Number Two appears on the scene, is quite upset with the interrogation, and scolds The Doctor harshly. Number Two reminds The Doctor that Number Six is too valuable for this kind of treatment. The Doctor submits to Number Two's authority.

Number Six awakens in his dwelling, apparently unaware of what has happened to him. After going through his morning routines, a maid in a "new dress" arrives with breakfast. A postman brings an invitation to a "carnival" that will be held that evening. Number Six walks outside and chats with Number Two, who extends a personal invitation to the carnival. Number Two then introduces Number Six to a woman who is charged with the duty of observing him. Number Six asks her questions but gets no response other than "Questions are a burden to others; answers are a prison for oneself." The observer leaves in a huff. Number Six tries to follow her but eventually returns home, befriending a black cat along the way.

The medical experiments become more brutal and more sadistic as the series progresses.

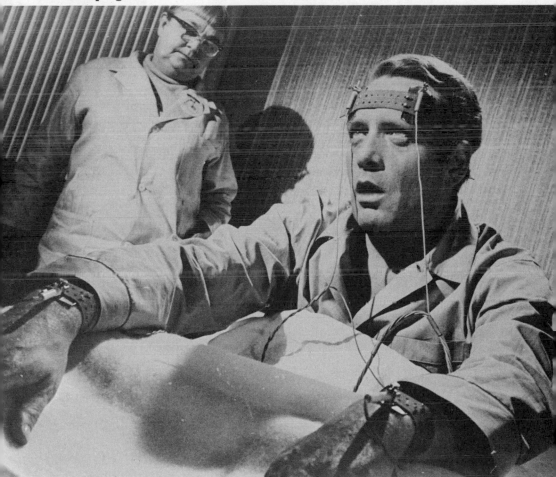

That night Number Six refuses to sleep. Instead he breaks out of his dwelling and heads to the beach. After dodging Rover a few times, he falls asleep. On waking, he spots a dead man washed up on the shore. He goes through the man's belongings and finds a wallet and a transistor radio.

Number Six returns to his dwelling and eventually climbs to the top of the bell tower to play the transistor radio. The radio plays in various languages. Finally he finds an English-language station, which is broadcasting a cryptic message about liberty. The last line he hears is "Only through pain can tomorrow be ensured." Unfortunately, Number Six was being watched in all this by his observer, and she and Number Two soon scale the bell tower. Number Two confiscates the radio and warns Number Six about obeying the rules. Number Six is now very aware that the woman is watching all his moves.

Number Six goes to the beach, grabs a life preserver, and walks cautiously into a cave. In the cave is the body of the dead man, as if it had been placed there. Number Six writes a note and combines it with a photograph of himself, inserting both items into the coat of the dead man. He then drags the dead man—who is now wearing the life preserver—into the sea. After he has dumped the body, he becomes aware of a man standing behind him, at the opening of the cave. That man is his old friend and colleague, Dutton. They converse. Number Six learns that Dutton has told the authorities everything he knows, and that he—Dutton—is now expendable. He is waiting for death.

That evening Number Six (dressed in his tuxedo) meets Number Two at the beach (who is dressed like Peter Pan). The two of them go to the carnival together. When Number Six spots the proper opportunity, he slips out of the carnival. He puts on a lab coat and starts walking down the corridors, trying to open doors. He continues opening doors that shouldn't be opened until he finds a morgue. He opens a drawer to discover the body of the dead man that had been dragged into the sea. Upon this discovery, Number Six sees the black cat. Behind the black cat is Number Two, who claims the cat as her pet and confidante. Number Two informs Number Six that they had intercepted the dead body and replaced the written note with one of their own. This new note claimed that Number Six himself was dead. Number Six is asked to rejoin the carnival.

When Number Six returns, the carnival appears to have ended, and the room is set up for an inquisition. Number Six is forced to stand trial before three judges. He is charged with having in his possession a transistor radio. Number Two will be his defender in this court of law. After hearing from all witnesses (including Dutton, who has lost his mind), the judges sentence Number Six to death. The carnival crowd, in full dress, cheers wildly. Number Six escapes the mob, who run after him.

Number Six has a pre-carnival face-off with Number Two, dressed like Peter Pan.

He ends up in a room with a Teletype machine that is frantically pumping out paper. He destroys it. Number Two enters. She admires Number Six's ingenuity but reminds him that, in the end, he will be forced to cooperate. As if to stress that point, the Teletype machine starts working again, spewing out more and more paper. As Number Two laughs, we see that the Teletype machine works even though its wires and inside parts have been pulled out.

OBSERVATIONS

- The strongest female character in any episode of *The Prisoner* is Mary Morris's role as Number Two in "Dance of the Dead." Because of Morris's strong role, and because of a supporting cast of females, this episode has been rightly or wrongly discussed as "the women's epi-

Number Six will be tried for the illegal use of a transistor radio. The Observer (dressed like Little Bo Peep) and Number Two take the matter very seriously.

sode." If we are to glean any insights into women from this episode, they would most likely be negative, especially with the infamous line delivered by Number Six: "Never trust a woman, even of the four-legged variety." Women in The Village are often portrayed as shallow observers, conspirators, or demagogues. And even the strength of Morris's role is undermined somewhat when you learn that the part was originally written for a man—for Trevor Howard, in fact.

• Many people argue that this episode was originally intended to be the second in the series. Such arguments certainly help explain some curious introductory dialogue (at one point, Number Six says flat out: "I'm new here"). However, there are equally strong arguments that "Free for All," "Checkmate," and "The Chimes of Big Ben" were each intended to be the second episode. The confusion about the proper second episode appears to come from the fact that four different screenwriters were probably working under the assumption that their assigned script was the second script. Each one had been handed the script for "Arrival" and told to come up with a new script for the series. Therefore, any one of the four could have been the second episode.

   While working on the series, the proper ordering of the episodes was not a critical concern of the filmmakers. This was a television series, after all, and few expected the ordering to be put to any kind of rigorous test. Once the series was about to air, however, decisions were made about sequential ordering. These decisions would have been made according to several factors: a balancing of those episodes that contained strong footage from The Village with episodes dominated by London footage, for example (and some of the episodes had not been completed when the series started to air, which would have forced them to be placed later in the series).

   "Dance of the Dead" was scheduled exceptionally late in the series, however—considering the fact that it was a potential candidate for the second episode. This probably had more to do with the final outcome of the episode than with any kind of balancing act. The plot of this episode is not only intricate but, in many ways, undisciplined and nonsensical, as evidenced in the synopsis above. It is primarily a montage of ideas, and the ideas are among the most powerful in the series: democratic values, justice, and the structure of authority. Considering the difficulty that a viewer faces when trying to put the pieces together, it makes sense that the episode would be pushed back in the sequential order. You need some basis in the series before you can attempt to understand this episode—or even enjoy it.

• Like the first episode of the series, Number Six is often played like a caged animal—angry, stubborn, temperamental. At one point Number

Two tries to make sense of it all with the double entendre "He's an individual . . . and they're always trying."

- There is evidence of sadism and torture in this episode—the first time we've seen it, but not the last (see "Hammer into Anvil"). At the opening of the episode, Number Six himself is undergoing a torturous scientific examination, until Number Two puts a stop to it. And there's evidence that Number Six's friend from home, Dutton, has gone through and will continue to go through torturous interrogation. If there is a message here, it is probably revealed in the broadcast over the transistor radio: "Only through pain can tomorrow be ensured."

- Number Six appears at a carnival dressed in a tuxedo and looking very much like John Drake of *Secret Agent*.

- There is irony in the fact that Number Six is judged for what we (and Number Two) know to be a minor crime (the possession of a transistor radio). Indeed, Number Six has broken more serious rules, the most serious of which would be trying to get a secret message out of The Village. The minor charge illustrates the absurdity of the court and its procedures. It appears that justice is more a matter of theatrics, played for the bloodthirst of the mob, than a method of getting to the truth or righting a wrong.

- During the carnival, several interesting costumes are worn. Number Six, as mentioned, wears a suit. Number Six's observer is dressed like Little Bo Peep. The Doctor is dressed like Napoleon. Dutton is dressed like a court jester. And Number Two plays Peter Pan. If Trevor Howard (or any man) had played the role of Number Two, he was to be dressed like Jack the Ripper.

- The props that were requested for this episode included "three breakfast trays; coffeepot; cups, etc.; silverware; village scroll for town crier; old-fashioned town crier's handbell; transistor radio—no named makers (this radio is wet from body in sea); tubs of village ice cream wrapped in polythene bags; flags of all nationalities (hand flags); soggy plain lifebelt and rope; clipboard; stopwatch; pen; pipe; soggy wet tobacco pouch; billfold type of wallet containing photo of the dead young man and pretty girl; paper; invitation cards for carnival; black surgical bag and walking stick as for 'Jack the Ripper'* dummy body to float in sea; cafe dressing; paintbrushes; paint; shovels; spades."

- The actress who played Number Six's observer, Norma West, has discussed McGoohan's state of mind at the time this episode was produced.

*Jack the Ripper props were intended for Trevor Howard as Number Two; the costuming was changed for Mary Morris's role as Peter Pan.

Number Six wears no costume to the carnival, but instead wears this tuxedo, making him look very much like John Drake of *Secret Agent*.

In an interview conducted by Tony Worrall, she said, "He was in a state of exhaustion, and really refusing at that stage to delegate responsibility. He was taking everything on himself even down to composing the music. He never went home—he slept in his dressing room and hardly ate."

"DO NOT FORSAKE ME OH MY DARLING": EPISODE NINE

Writer: Vincent Tilsley
Script Editor: George Markstein
Producer: David Tomblin
Director: Pat Jackson
Executive Producer: Patrick McGoohan

CAST

Patrick McGoohan (Number Six), Zena Walker (Janet), Clifford Evans (Number Two), Nigel Stock (The Colonel), Angelo Muscat (The Butler), Hugo Schuster (Seltzman), John Wentworth (Sir Charles), James Bree (Villiers), Lloyd Lamble (Stapleton), Patrick Jordan (Danvers), Lockwood West (Camera Shop Manager), Frederic Abbott (Potter), Gertan Klauber (Cafe Waiter), Henry Longhurst (Old Guest), Danvers Walker (First New Man), John Nolan (Young Guest).

CREW

Ronald Liles (Production Manager), Brendan J. Stafford (Director of Photography), Jack Shampan (Art Director), Len Harris (Camera Operator), Eric Boyd-Perkins (Editor), Ron Grainer (Musical Theme), Albert Elms (Musical Director), Gino Marotta, Ernie Lewis (Assistant Directors), Wilfred Thompson (Sound Editor), John Bramall (Sound Recordist), Eric Mival (Music Editor), Rose Tobias-Shaw (Casting Director), Ann Besserman (Continuity), Colin Southcott (Set Dresser), Frank Turner (Makeup), Olive Mills (Hairdressing), Dora Lloyd (Wardrobe), Jack Cooper (Flight Arranger).

SYNOPSIS

Various men, apparently British, sit around watching a slide show. They are trying to break some type of code. They believe that the code will lead them to a Dr. Seltzman. After many attempts they realize that the code cannot be broken—or perhaps no code exists at all.

A helicopter flies into The Village. Number Two welcomes The Colonel, who has just arrived in the helicopter. The Colonel does not know why he has been brought to The Village and is anxious to learn his assignment. Number Two discusses Dr. Seltzman with The Colonel. Apparently Dr. Seltzman was "a great neurologist who became fascinated with the study of thought transfers." He had developed a technology in

63

which "one man's mind could be placed in another man's body." The Village has one of Seltzman's machines, and The Colonel is given a demonstration. Number Two fantasizes about the espionage possibilities inherent in such a machine. Theoretically, during diplomatic swaps, they could place their men in top-security positions in other nations. With this power they could break the security of any nation. Although not stated overtly, The Colonel's assignment is to learn the whereabouts of Dr. Seltzman. He will do this by switching minds with Number Six.

The scenery changes. A man we believe to be Number Six wakes up, looks at his watch, looks at the picture of a woman, and then looks in the mirror. The face is not that of Number Six, but instead that of The Colonel. The switch has obviously taken place, but Number Six is confused. While looking in the mirror, he starts to recall some of the things that had happened to him. Suddenly the doorbell rings.

There's a woman named Janet at the door (the same woman who was in the photograph). She has noticed the Lotus 7 outside and thought that maybe "he" was here. Number Six knows Janet well but also knows that she can't recognize him in his current state of face. We learn from Janet that Number Six has been gone for over a year, and we also learn that Number Six used to work for Janet's father. It is also to be understood that Janet and Number Six were once lovers (it is later learned that they were, and probably still are, engaged to be married), and that she is in great distress over his disappearance. She leaves confused, unsure of who this man is or why the car is outside the door. Number Six smashes his fist in the mirror.

Number Six drives to his former offices and demands to see his old boss and future father-in-law, Sir Charles Portland. Number Six claims that his mind has been exchanged through one of Seltzman's devices, but Portland has trouble believing any of the story. He is intrigued enough, however, to hire a man to follow Number Six's every move. Before leaving, Portland asks if Seltzman perfected the reversion procedure and then remarks: "If he didn't, it's a pity."

That night Number Six goes uninvited to Janet's birthday party. He asks her to return to him a slip of paper that her fiancé had given her one year ago. She gives him the paper, still not sure whether to trust him or not. Outside, Number Six embraces Janet and kisses her long and lovingly. The kiss convinces her of his sincerity—that this man is indeed her fiancé. Number Six is strengthened by her faith.

The slip given to Number Six by Janet was a sales slip for photographs. Number Six goes to the camera store, claims the photographs, brings them to his apartment, and breaks the code. The photographs, when superimposed in the proper order, reveal a location: Kandersfeld, Austria. Number Six gets in his car, the Lotus 7, and drives to Kandersfeld, followed all the time by one of Portland's henchmen (and also, we suspect, by one of The Village's men). When he arrives in Kandersfeld, he locates Dr. Seltzman, who has taken on the job of the local barber. He convinces Seltzman that he is who he says he is. Seltzman agrees to try and reverse the process so Number Six's mind can be reunited with his body. After this short discussion Portland's henchman arrives, and a scuffle breaks out between Number Six and the henchman. It's all for naught, however, because the man from The Village arrives and gasses them both.

Seltzman and Number Six are brought to The Village. Number Two wants Seltzman to reveal the secrets of the reversal process. Seltzman agrees, under one condition: that he be left alone during the laboratory work. Number Two agrees but asks his assistants to take notes during the procedure. Seltzman wires up the electrodes to Number Six's head, his own head, and The Colonel's head. The electricity starts sparking

Number Six, whose mind is inhabiting this new body, looks lovingly at his fiancée, Janet.

among the three heads, and Seltzman collapses. The Colonel stands up, is commended on his work, and is allowed to leave the village by helicopter. After he leaves, Seltzman says, "You assured me he was in good health. You must tell Number One I did my duty." It becomes apparent that The Colonel's mind has been transmitted into Seltzman's body, that Seltzman's was transmitted into The Colonel's body, and that Number Six is Number Six, of sound mind and body. It is also apparent that Seltzman, in The Colonel's body, has successfully escaped from The Village. Number Six sits up and says before a very shaken Number Two: "He can and did change three minds at the same time. He is free to continue his experiments in peace."

OBSERVATIONS

• The original production schedule of *The Prisoner* was reportedly set up to handle the production of twenty-six individual episodes, and that schedule called for two intensive work periods, each of which would produce thirteen episodes. It became apparent during the filming of the first thirteen episodes, however, that the idea could not be sustained over twenty-six episodes, and thus a compromise was struck: seventeen episodes would be produced, and the production schedule that originally was set for thirteen episodes would be extended to complete seventeen episodes. There was a problem with this extended scheduling, however: many of the production personnel had made other commitments and could not stay on for this extension period. And one of the big stars of the series had himself made a commitment: Patrick McGoohan was to be in Hollywood for the filming of *Ice Station Zebra*. The episode that got stuck in the middle of all this schedule chaos was "Do Not Forsake Me Oh My Darling," and it's all the better for it.

   Considering that McGoohan was unable to star in this episode, a novel script was created that called for McGoohan's mind to be placed in another man's body. It was a creative decision made of necessity and provided for one of the more fascinating episodes in the series. The episode we see, however, is not the episode as first conceived. When McGoohan returned from Hollywood, he was reportedly quite upset; he shot new scenes and reedited the entire episode.

• This episode played as the thirteenth on its first airing in Great Britain. It was played as the ninth episode overseas, including in the United States. Apparently, considering the extensive editing that was discussed above, this episode was not ready to air when the ninth episode was first shown. It was thus pushed back in Great Britain but aired in proper order overseas (or at least proper in terms of the production company's press sheets).

- Somebody actually escapes in this episode, and the person is a major scientist. Holding fast to the idea that "the problem with science is that it can be perverted," there is nonetheless an incredible respect for Dr. Seltzman in this episode.

- We learn a lot about Number Six's former life in this episode, the most important of which is the revelation of his engagement to Janet. We also learn a few of the code names he operated under as a secret agent: Duvall in France, Schmidt in Germany, and the general code number ZM73.

- In this episode Number Six proves his identity by comparing his hand-writing with a letter he had addressed to Dr. Seltzman over a year ago. The handwriting is McGoohan's own. The address of the letter—Port-meirion Road—is the first clue that audiences had as to the actual location of The Village. (We now know that The Village exterior scenes were shot at the Portmeirion Resort in North Wales, but that was a highly guarded secret during the first broadcast of the show.)

- Although it is difficult to tell even with freeze frames, it appears that the dollar bills locked away in Number Six's safe are United States dollars. Does this mean that Number Six has some connection to the U.S. government, or does it simply mean that he has more faith in the stability of the dollar than he does in the British pound?

- This is the only episode that has any affectionate embrace between Number Six and a woman. Number Six's mind is in another body, so Patrick McGoohan was not directly involved in the love scene. It has been mentioned by at least one co-star that McGoohan had a problem with physical intimacy on the set. Perhaps that's why most of the love scenes were written out of other scripts (both "The Chimes of Big Ben" and "Many Happy Returns" originally called for at least one "kiss-ing" scene). McGoohan has defended his editing of such scenes to ensure that the series be good, wholesome, family entertainment.

"IT'S YOUR FUNERAL": EPISODE TEN

Writer: Michael Cramoy
Script Editor: George Markstein
Producer: David Tomblin
Director: Robert Asher
Executive Producer: Patrick McGoohan

CAST
Patrick McGoohan (Number Six), Derren Nesbitt (New Number Two), Annette Andre (Watchmaker's Daughter), Mark Eden (Number One Hundred), Andre Van Gyseghem (Retiring Number Two), Martin Miller (Watchmaker), Wanda Ventham (Computer Attendant), Angelo Muscat (The Butler), Mark Burns (Number Two's Assistant), Peter Swanwick (Supervisor), Charles Lloyd Pack (Artist), Grace Arnold (Number Thirty-six), Arthur White (Stall Holder), Michael Bilton (M. C. Councillor), Gerry Crampton (Kosho Opponent).

CREW
Bernard Williams (Production Manager), Brendan J. Stafford (Director of Photography), Jack Shampan (Art Director), Jack Lowin (Camera Operator), John S. Smith (Editor), Ron Grainer (Musical Theme), Albert Elms (Musical Director), Gino Marotta (Assistant Director), Ken Rolls (Sound Editor), John Bramall (Sound Recordist), John S. Smith (Music Editor), Doris Martin (Continuity), Kenneth Bridgeman (Set Dresser), Eddie Knight (Makeup), Pat McDermot (Hairdressing), Masada Wilmot (Wardrobe).

SYNOPSIS
A woman enters Number Six's dwelling in the morning, with Number Six still asleep. She wakes him. Number Six is suspicious, and rightly so: every movement is being monitored on the screen by Number Two and his assistants. The woman passes out. Number Six discovers that she is under the influence of some drug. He revives her and agrees to talk with her. She talks about an assassination attempt and discusses the activities of "jammers." Number Six refuses to take her seriously. She storms out of his room.

Number Two is not only monitoring this meeting, but he planned it—right down to the detail of her passing out. The woman, without knowledge, had been manipulated by special drugs. He's not totally satisfied with the result of the meeting, however, and it's obvious that

Number Fifty has a difficult time convincing Number Six that she's not working for Number Two.

some plan is under way. Number Two discusses the plan with a higher authority on the telephone.

Number Six learns more details about "jamming" from an artist. It's an act of protest, a kind of civil disobedience. People with no plans to revolt against society nonetheless act as if they have such plans. The authorities are forced to check out the plots. It's a nuisance, and it wastes the authorities' time.

The New Number Two is quite amused by Number Six's warning of assassination. Number Six will have the last laugh.

Number Two monitors the daily activities of Number Six, which includes a game of kosho. While Number Six is engaged in this strange trampoline game, Number One Hundred—on assignment from Number Two—secretly removes Number Six's watch from his locker and replaces it with another. After the game Number Six realizes his watch doesn't work, and he makes his way to the watchmaker's shop. At the shop, Number Six notices an explosive detonating device on the shelf. He's curious but gets no response from the watchmaker.

He learns later that the watchmaker is the father of the woman who entered his room during the morning. The woman confides to Number Six that her father is involved in an assassination plot, and that the intended victim is Number Two. Number Six becomes concerned. He pays a visit to the watchmaker and, with the daughter, tries to talk the man out of his violent plan. Number Six believes that everyone in The Village will be punished for the mad act of an old man. Number Two and Number One Hundred watch the exchange on a monitor and appear quite pleased.

Number Six feels compelled to warn Number Two about the assassination plans. But Number Two acts as if he finds the whole idea humorous—another innocent plot by the harmless jammers. Getting no satisfaction, Number Six storms out of the office. Number Two has not only expected this to happen, he has filmed the entire meeting. Indeed, everything is going according to plan.

Number Six learns that a major ceremony will be held on Appreciation Day, and that the watchmaker has implanted an explosive device in a medallion that will be placed over the neck of Number Two during the ceremony. With this knowledge, he makes one more attempt to convince Number Two of the plot. However, when Number Six enters the offices of Number Two, he sees an elderly man in control—not the young man he had spoken to earlier. This older man recognizes Number Six immediately, identifies himself as Number Two, and says he understands that Number Six is there to issue an assassination warning. Number Two adds that he's been advised about Number Six's warnings by the "acting" Number Two. However, Number Six is able to convince this Number Two that danger does exist. But that doesn't stop the assassination attempt. Number Two resigns himself to the inevitability of his death, saying, "You never understood us, Number Six. We never fail."

The ceremony is held the next day. The Villagers come out. Bands play. Anticipation is high. The great ritual is the passing of the medallion (called The Seal) from the old Number Two to the new Number Two. The watchmaker is in the bell tower, under instructions to blow up the old Number Two once the medallion is around his neck. Number Six finds the watchmaker, however, and confiscates the remote-control exploding device. The tension mounts. At one point in the ceremony, the

The Old Number Two prepares to escape the abuses of power and the finality of old age.

old Number Two places the seal over the neck of the new Number Two. The new Number Two sweats it out, thinking very possibly that he will be blown to bits. Number Six returns to the ceremony, hands the exploding device to the old Number Two, and encourages him to fly to freedom in The Village helicopter. No one will stop him as long as he holds the device and the new Number Two wears the dangerous seal. The escape is successful, and Number Six can't resist giving a few sarcastic remarks to the new Number Two, now that his plot has failed.

OBSERVATIONS

• Number Two has accurately identified a weakness within Number Six, and that is his real compassion for women in distress. It is, in the end, a heroic quality of long standing—chivalric, in a way. Although Number Two plays on this tendency, it is a very human quality that makes Number Six all the more attractive.

• This episode provides many sympathetic portrayals of The Villagers— people who apparently want to escape, want to maintain their dignity, and are willing to go to violent extremes in order to at least protest their situation. These noble acts of individualism, however, have been

Number Six, having the last laugh. Note the explosive seal around the neck of the New Number Two.

encouraged by the authorities for their own internal purposes. What's most interesting about this somewhat confusing episode is not that The Villagers have shown a sense of solidarity, but that chaos reigns among the authorities.

• This is a serious episode, with little humor. Its message is subtle and complex, and it is confounded by a plotline that is often confusing and difficult to follow. The ideas are noble, however: Number Six, always able to cut to the heart of the matter, understands that The Villagers are going to be blamed and punished for an assassination that is being plotted by the authorities themselves. The only way to prevent the unjust punishment is to prevent the violent act. Although Number Six succeeds in his mission, there is something of a letdown in the fact that the assassination is not successful—after all, it is an act against authority, and we've been set up during the program for an explosion that never occurs. But this episode concerns what is ultimately good for us, not what stimulates us at the present. It's a cerebral victory.

• The idea of age is very much a part of this episode. An old Number Two is going to be assassinated because he is no longer useful to the authorities—and may be dangerous. An old man, a watchmaker, becomes an unwitting accomplice to an assassination plot.

• In many ways, this episode attacks the effectiveness of violent protest, which is especially interesting in light of its being a product of the late 1960s. The clearest exchange of ideas addresses this:

Watchmaker: What I am doing is for a principle. We are in this prison for life. All of us. But I have met no one here who has committed a crime. I will protest in a manner they cannot ignore.

Number Six: Some other way, then. Not by an act of murder.

Watchmaker: (Correcting) Assassination.

Number Six: Call it what you like. The important matter is that the entire village will be punished.

Watchmaker: Maybe it is what they need to wake them up. To shake them out of their lethargy. To make them angry enough to fight.

Number Six: That's assuming they survive the punishment.

• This episode seems to be strongly aligned with nonviolent protest. However, it is hard to reconcile this episode with the orgiastic, chaotic violence that is to come in "Fall Out." There appears to be some ambivalence about the proper role of violence in revolt.

"CHECKMATE": EPISODE ELEVEN

Writer: Gerald Kelsey
Script Editor: George Markstein
Producer: David Tomblin
Director: Don Chaffey
Executive Producer: Patrick McGoohan

CAST

Patrick McGoohan (Number Six), Ronald Radd (Rook), Patricia Jessel (1st Psychiatrist), Peter Wyngarde (Number Two), Rosalie Crutchley (The Queen), George Coulouris (Man with the Stick), Angelo Muscat (The Butler), Bee Duffell (2nd Psychiatrist), Basil Dignam (Supervisor), Danvers Walker (Painter), Denis Shaw (Shopkeeper), Victor Platt (Assistant Supervisor), Shivaun O'Casey (Nurse), Geoffrey Reed (Skipper), Terence Donovan (Sailor), Joe Dunne (1st Tower Guard), Romo Gorrara (2nd Tower Guard).

CREW

Bernard Williams (Production Manager), Brendan J. Stafford (Director of Photography), Jack Shampan (Art Director), Jack Lowin (Camera Operator), Lee Doig (Editor), Ron Grainer (Musical Theme), Robert Monks (2nd Unit Cameraman), Gino Marotta (Assistant Director), Clive Smith (Sound Editor), John Bramall (Sound Recordist), Bob Dearberg (Music Editor), Rose Tobias-Shaw (Casting Director), Doris Martin (Continuity), Kenneth Bridgeman (Set Dresser), Eddie Knight (Makeup), Pat McDermot (Hairdressing), Masada Wilmot (Wardrobe).

SYNOPSIS

Number Six notices a street full of Villagers, walking around actively. Suddenly they freeze in their tracks. Rover is bounding down the street. A man with a walking stick, however, is apparently immune to Rover's freeze-frame effect. He continues to walk, inattentive to the surrounding oddity. Number Six is intrigued. He follows the man. On greeting him, the man asks if Number Six will join him in a game of chess. Number Six agrees, only to learn that the game of chess is played with real people on an enormous board. Number Six plays The Queen's pawn, and learns from The Queen a little about the man with the stick, who is calling the moves over a megaphone. The man is understood to be an ex-count, and this game has been played by his ancestors for generations.

During the game, a man playing The Rook does the unthinkable: he moves himself to a position on the board and yells, "Check," without any instructions from the man or his opponent. This forbidden "cult of the individual" causes a flurry of mad activity. The Rook is taken away in an ambulance, and the game quickly ends. After the game, Number Six engages the man with a stick in conversation. From this man he learns that it is possible to tell the common Villagers from the authorities. You must "judge by attitudes." Number Six intuits that the common Villagers are easily intimidated and will generally follow any orders given to them without complaint. The authorities are arrogant and unwilling to cooperate. From this knowledge he finally has a way of determining whom to trust.

The Queen is obviously attracted to Number Six, and she tries to engage him in a postgame discussion. Number Six is cool to her, however, and is intent on finding out what happened to The Rook. The Rook is in the hospital, being subjected to electrical shock treatments based on Pavlov's experiments. These are to make him behave. After The Rook is released from the hospital, Number Six befriends him and starts to plot an escape. It is obvious that Number Six is starting to put his theory into

One of the favorite activities at The Village is a good game of chess.

The Rook is guilty of adhering to the "cult of the individual."

action. He's found a formula for trust, and he trusts The Rook. The Rook, however, appears somewhat suspicious of Number Six.

The authorities know that Number Six is up to something, but they aren't too concerned. For insurance purposes, they brainwash The Queen into believing that she and Number Six are desperately in love. They then put a remote-control device in a locket that is held around her neck. The theory behind this is that The Queen will follow Number Six wherever he goes, and thus the authorities will always know the whereabouts of Number Six.

Meanwhile, Number Six has been gathering cohorts for his escape attempt, now that he believes he knows whom he can trust. We watch as he and The Rook enlist two men, a painter and a shopkeeper. Number Six has an escape plan, and the others play their parts. The Rook will build a radio that can make contact with ships in the ocean. They will send a distress signal, as if they were a plane about to crash. All they need is a transistor to complete their electronic signaling device. They get the transistor when Number Six discovers the locket around the neck of a very pesty Queen. He takes the locket, which serves two purposes: it helps them build their device, and it thwarts the surveillance of the authorities. Success seems imminent.

They do get reaction from their distress (May day) signal: a boat just off the coast answers their call. The Rook wades out to sea in a raft with the distress signal, hoping that it will lure the boat into land, after which the conspirators can be picked up. Number Six instructs the other conspirators (who now include the man with a stick and another anonymous Villager) to help him capture and disarm Number Two—the only person who can successfully thwart their attempt. They do so. While capturing Number Two, something seems to go wrong. The raft on which The Rook was wading has drifted back to shore, unmanned. Number Six gets on the raft, goes out to sea, scouts the rescue boat, and is brought on board. Once safe, he suddenly sees Number Two—who was supposed to be tied up—on a television monitor. Beside Number Two is The Rook. The Rook has foiled the plan, evidently because he believed Number Six to be an authority, not a prisoner. Number Two jokes that Number Six was caught by his own trap: he exhibited too much arrogance for the other prisoners to trust him. Number Six desperately tries to escape but fails.

OBSERVATIONS

- In no other episode do we get such a sympathetic portrayal of the individuals confined within The Village. Apparently there are numerous Villagers who harbor individual thoughts of escape. Number Six may be unsuccessful in rallying them to his cause, but they do think and, in certain situations, are even willing to buck authority.

The Queen is quite taken by her very dapper pawn.

- The only person not frozen by Rover's presence at the beginning of this episode is the man with a stick (who is a descendant of royal lineage). Unlike most people who refuse to freeze, this man walks deliberately onward, and Rover passes him by. No reason is ever given for the immunity of this man to Rover's power, but it gives further ammunition to the theory that certain men are by nature supermen—endowned with a uniqueness of mind that separates them from the masses.

- Number Six's dictate to "never trust a woman" is followed rigorously in this episode, and with reason. The Queen, a woman who has been programmed to love and faithfully follow Number Six, makes many honest attempts to gain his confidence, only to be scorned and forgotten. She has been programmed to "protect" Number Six, in much the same way that a queen in the game of chess can protect a pawn. Indeed, the original name of this episode—changed at the last minute—was "The Queen's Pawn." (It should be noted that while Number Six doesn't trust women, he is very willing to protect them;

as Number Two notes in "A Change of Mind," he's a sucker for a damsel in distress.)

- The script, written by Gerald Kelsey, is among the best in the entire series, making good use of many standard *Prisoner* locations and personalities. It is considered by many to be the quintessential *Prisoner* episode, and Patrick McGoohan considers it one of the "original seven."

- Number Two is seen meditating in one of the scenes and then, like a martial artist, splitting a piece of wood in two with his bare hands. The script in this episode calls for the meditative trance but not for the splitting of the wood, which must have been improvised on the set. The script reads: "Number Two is sitting cross-legged on the floor in the manner and garb of one engaged in Yogi exercises." This scene is representative of the various ways in which 1960s culture permeates the world of *The Prisoner*.

- There is a nice moment in this episode when Number Six is engaged in a psychological test concerning word association. The banter goes like this:

Woman: Cat.
Number Six: Dog.
Woman: Rain.
Number Six: Shine.
Woman: Desk.
Number Six: Work.
Woman: Hope.
Number Six: Anchor.
Woman: Anchor?
Number Six: Hope and Anchor: pub I used to drink at.
Woman: Tree.
Number Six: Leaf.
Woman: Home.
Number Six: Away.
Woman: Return.
Number Six: Game.
Woman: Love.
Number Six: Game.
Woman: Game?
Number Six: Tennis.
Woman: Table.
Number Six: Chair.
Woman: Ship.
Number Six: Shape.

Woman: Red.
Number Six: Sails.
Woman: Free.
Number Six: For all.

- Two very famous experiments are played out on The Villagers in this episode. The Rook is subjected to Pavlovian experiments, designed to condition behavior through positive and negative response (in this case, a thirsty Rook has to drink from the proper-colored water cooler in order to avoid electrical shock). The other experiment, performed on The Queen, turns the subject into a homing device. As the psychiatrist tells it, this experiment was originally performed with dolphins for military purposes (it turns the good intentions of the subject—in this case, the love of The Queen—into a method of sabotage). The authorities in The Village appear very willing to treat their subjects like animals.

- Life is like a game of chess, with authorities calling the moves. The game of chess plays a dominant symbolic role throughout the series.

- The Rook, before he was incarcerated, had invented an "electronic defense system." He was brought to The Village because, in the name of peace, he felt that all nations should have the technology. Perhaps the inventors of the Star Wars defense system were *Prisoner* fans?

"LIVING IN HARMONY": EPISODE TWELVE

Writer: David Tomblin
From a story by: David Tomblin and Ian L. Rakoff
Producer: David Tomblin
Director: David Tomblin
Executive Producer: Patrick McGoohan

CAST

Patrick McGoohan (Number Six), Alexis Kanner (The Kid), David Bauer (The Judge), Valerie French (Cathy), Gordon Tanner (Town Elder), Gordon Sterne (Bystander), Michael Balfour (Will), Larry Taylor (Mexican Sam), Monti de Lyle (Town Dignitary), Douglas Jone (Horse Dealer), Bill Nick (1st Gunman), Les Crawford (2nd Gunman), Frank Maher (3rd Gunman), Max Faulkner (1st Horseman), Bill Cummings (2nd Horseman), Eddie Eddon (3rd Horseman).

CREW

Ronald Liles (Production Manager), Brendan J. Stafford (Director of Photography), Jack Shampan (Art Director), Len Harris (Camera Operator), Noreen Ackland (Editor), Ron Grainer (Musical Theme), Albert Elms (Musical Director), Gino Marotta (Assistant Director), Wilfred Thompson (Sound Editor), Cyril Swern (Sound Recordist), Eric Mival (Music Editor), Rose Tobias-Shaw (Casting Director), John Lageu (Set Dresser), Phyllis Townshend (Continuity), Frank Turner (Makeup), Olive Mills (Hairdressing), Dora Lloyd (Wardrobe).

SYNOPSIS

Number Six is dressed in cowboy garb. He turns in a sheriff's badge, unstraps his gun holster, and drops the gun and holster on The Marshall's desk. Several western thugs beat him up, and when he awakens he is in the town of Harmony. The Judge in Harmony offers him a job as sheriff. Number Six impolitely refuses the position. He then makes a few sarcastic remarks about the town. The townspeople become upset at what they consider to be insults. The Judge has Number Six locked up in prison, for protective custody.

In jail, Number Six meets two characters. The first is an angry thug known as The Kid, and he is charged with guarding Number Six. He obviously doesn't like Number Six and talks loud and tough. The other character is Kathy, a woman who helps Number Six escape from the jail by giving him the keys and getting The Kid too drunk to care. Kathy's brother had just been hung, and she may want Number Six to help her avenge the death. Number Six escapes but is captured along the way and brought back for trial.

The trial, set in the saloon, is not to judge Number Six but instead to judge Kathy, who helped Number Six escape. Kathy is found guilty and put in the local jail. The Judge tells Number Six that Kathy will be freed if Number Six agrees to become the sheriff. To complicate the matter, The Judge assigns The Kid to guard Kathy, and Number Six is very aware that The Kid tends to get "overaffectionate." Number Six

Number Six finds himself a stranger in the town of Harmony.

succumbs to the pressure. He wears the badge of sheriff, and Kathy is freed.

Number Six agrees to wear the badge but not the gun. After many physical attempts to break their new sheriff, the townspeople are impressed: Number Six may be able to survive without a gun. The Kid, however, continues to cause problems. He is obviously jealous of Kathy's interest in Number Six, and he shoots dead another man who was flirting with Kathy. The townspeople feel that it's time for the sheriff to take up a gun. They want to clean up the town of people like The Kid but note that "we can't do it alone, and, Sheriff, neither can you."

The Judge conspires to force a gun into Number Six's hand. He makes The Kid aware of Kathy's affections for Number Six. The Kid finds Kathy alone in the saloon and plays out a jealous rage. When he forces a kiss on Kathy, she bites him hard on the lip. He explodes and kills her. After burying Kathy, Number Six does take up a gun and engages in a stand-off gunfight with The Kid. Number Six kills him easily, returns to the saloon, and informs The Judge that he's leaving the town. The Judge (who only wanted The Kid to "rough" Kathy up a little) will hear none of it, and Number Six is forced into a shootout with The Judge's men. The Judge eventually shoots Number Six in the back and kills him dead.

Number Six awakens and finds himself dressed in Village clothes, with headphones on. The western town around him is empty, filled with cardboard cutouts of the townspeople. Number Six finally confronts The Judge, The Kid, and Kathy, who are actually Number Two, Number Eight, and Number Twenty-two. Number Two is upset that his experiment—which involved hallucinogenic drugs—didn't work. Number Twenty-two starts to cry, apparently upset over her role in this manipulation of Number Six. Suddenly Number Eight begins to play out his role again as The Kid. He becomes jealous of Kathy's sympathy for Number Six and follows her out to the saloon. He strangles her, and she dies in Number Six's arms. Number Eight, still acting like The Kid, makes a mad attempt to confront Number Six. He climbs to the top of a balcony and then jumps over the rails, killing himself. Number Six surveys the situation, gone fundamentally wrong. He walks out of the saloon.

OBSERVATIONS

- This episode has the distinction of being the only one that was not aired in the United States during the initial broadcast run, owing to censorship problems. There have been many theories as to why this specific episode caused so much concern. A network censor cited the drug-related aspects to the program, although this seems somewhat difficult to believe considering the fact that over half the episodes concern drugs. A more pertinent reason is probably the refusal of Number Six to arm himself in defense of the community; remember that this was at the height of the Vietnam War. Indeed, an ITC official has stated that this was the major concern of the U.S. broadcasters. It may also be that the setting of this episode—a small American town in the western tradition—hit a little close to home. It's easy enough to overlook potentially subversive ideas when they are proclaimed in a fantasy world like The Village, but when they are enacted within a mythical western town, they take on a keener sense of reality. In many ways, however, the setting was simply chosen to let McGoohan play out a fantasy—he always wanted to star in a western. There's a lot behind this censorship decision, which is discussed in detail in "The Great Debates."

There are many similarities between Patrick McGoohan's role as Number Six in this episode and Clint Eastwood's role as The Man With No Name in *The Good, the Bad, and the Ugly*.

- In several previous episodes we have seen Number Six act compassionately to fellow Villagers in trouble. In this episode the authorities play on that compassion as if it were a flaw. Number Six has been set up: a woman is apparently in trouble, and Number Six acts to right the wrongs. When it is learned at the end that the woman was in on the scheme from the beginning, it hurts. But it's important to point out that the woman herself sheds a tear—humbled and ashamed at what she had done.

- Alexis Kanner has a big role in this episode, and he will have an even more important role in the final episode, "Fall Out." There should be no attempt to see any similarity between the roles.

- Comparisons are easily made between this episode and the spaghetti westerns that were coming out of Italy at the same time, especially those directed by Sergio Leone and starring Clint Eastwood (*A Fistful of Dollars*, *For a Few Dollars More*, and the rest). Neither of the lead characters has a name. The musical score is also in the character of the spaghetti westerns. But they have very different attitudes toward violence and bloodshed. Number Six is like the western characters of the 1950s, something like Shane: a man who knows how to use a gun but only takes it up when he's forced to. The Man With No Name of the spaghetti westerns had but one ethic, and that was money.

"A CHANGE OF MIND:" EPISODE THIRTEEN

Writer: Roger Parkes
Script Editor: George Markstein
Producer: David Tomblin
Director: Joseph Serf
Executive Producer: Patrick McGoohan

CAST

Patrick McGoohan (Number Six), Angela Browne (Number Eighty-six), John Sharpe (Number Two), Angelo Muscat (The Butler), George Pravda (Doctor), Kathleen Breck (Number Forty-two), Peter Swanwick (Supervisor), Thomas Heathcote (Lobo Man), Bartlett Mullins (Committee Chairman), Michael Miller (Number Ninety-three), Joseph Cuby (1st Member of Social Group), Michael Chow (2nd Member of Social Group), June Ellis (Number Forty-Eight), John Hamblin (1st Woodland Man), Michael Billington (2nd Woodland Man).

CREW

Bernard Williams (Production Manager), Brendan J. Stafford (Director of Photography), Jack Shampan (Art Director), Jack Lowin (Camera Operator), Lee Doig (Editor), Ron Grainer (Musical Theme), Albert Elms (Musical Director), Gino Marotta (Assistant Director), Wilfred Thompson (Sound Editor), John Bramall (Sound Recordist), Eric Mival (Music Editor), Rose Tobias-Shaw (Casting Director), Doris Martin (Continuity), Kenneth Bridgeman (Set Dresser), Eddie Knight (Makeup), Pat McDermot (Hairdressing), Masada Wilmot (Wardrobe).

SYNOPSIS

Number Six works out at his private, homemade, outdoor gymnasium. A couple of Villagers come and taunt Number Six, calling him antisocial; they threaten that he'll have to face "the committee" for his behavior. Number Six is indeed called before the committee, and his antisocial actions are discussed. They inform Number Six that he is under investigation, and that he must conform. While walking out of the woods and into The Village, Number Two passes several Villagers who hold him in contempt. He reads an article in the *Tally Ho* that is headlined COMMITTEE CONTINUES HEARINGS. He arrives home to meet a fat Number Two, who sits there eating crackers and stressing the seriousness of the situation. Number Two warns that "if the hearings go against you, I am powerless to help you." A woman, Number Eighty-six, is assigned to Number Six—to help him "join in the group spirit."

Outside, Number Six observes a gathering of Villagers who are discussing "social conversion." They are militant, and Number Six, in character, engages in a battle of wits. The Villagers are not amused; they call him several names (a reactionary, a rebel, disharmonious) and break up their meeting. Number Six is then brought to the hospital for a physical. He witnesses various brutal experiments going on in the Aversion Therapy Room. The subjects of these experiments appear to have had some type of brain operation, judging from the strange scars on

Number Two warns Number Six that, if he doesn't conform, Number Two will be powerless to help him.

their heads. Number Six learns that such experiments are conducted on people who have been classified as "unmutual." He also learns that he will be subjected to "instant social conversion" if one more complaint is lodged against him.

The people of The Village turn their collective backs on Number Six. The loudspeakers ask Villagers to report on Number Six's antisocial activities; the newspaper prints damning editorials; and the waiters at the cafe will not even serve Number Six a cup of coffee. Eventually the community groups together and confronts him. They demand that he be hospitalized. They force him out of his dwelling and carry him to the hospital.

In the hospital Number Six is tranquilized and then put through what appears to be a brain-deadening ordeal. The Villagers are invited to watch this experiment over closed-circuit television. Those who do watch are introduced to the procedure by Number Eighty-six, who explains that the experiment will cause "dislocation of the aggressive frontal lobe of the brain." Every nuance of this procedure, involving various types of noises and light beams, is demonstrated.

Number Six wakes up in the hospital with a small bandage on his head. He is "cured." He leaves the hospital to the cheers of Villagers, all of whom believe that he has been forcibly socialized. Number Six himself is groggy and smiles benevolently. At home, Number Eighty-six prepares a cup of tea for Number Six. While Number Six is watching on the sly, she drops a white tablet in the teacup. Number Six dumps the tea in a flowerpot, unbeknownst to Number Eighty-six. He then sleeps. He awakens to Number Two asking him about his resignation. Number Six is drugged, but not as much as Number Two thinks he is. Number Six doesn't talk.

We learn from Number Two that the operation was a masquerade. The authorities wanted Number Six to think he was "lobotomized" when in fact he was not. The drugs are supposed to make Number Six passive and ready to talk. But Number Six is showing aggressive tendencies, much to the distress of Number Two, who insists that Number Six be pumped full of more drugs. On the next attempt Number Six outsmarts them. He exchanges teacups with Number Eighty-six. Number Eighty-six drinks from the drugged cup and loses it: she becomes all aflutter. Number Six seizes the opportunity. Understanding that he is in control of his faculties, he hypnotizes the drugged Number Eighty-six. She confirms the fact that the operation was a fake, and Number Six then plants his own suggestions in her mind. It has something to do with the fourth chime of The Village bells.

That afternoon Number Six volunteers to tell all to Number Two. But he insists that it be in a public forum: that he tell all The Villagers from the balcony of the town hall. Number Two readily agrees to this. Number Six starts talking to the masses, acting as if he is about to tell all. The chimes begin to ring. On the fourth chime Number Eighty-six stands out from the crowd, points to Number Two, and accuses him of being "unmutual." The crowd goes wild. Number Six encourages their anger. They storm toward Number Two, who is last seen being chased by an angry mob.

OBSERVATIONS

• This is the most unsympathetic portrayal of the common Villagers. They not only witlessly obey authority, they appear to take up the authoritative line as they would a cause and are quick to condemn those who do not conform. There is a mob mentality in this episode that is distinctly absent from any others. It's as if the entire community had been drugged, beaten, or otherwise conformed, which is distinctly possible. In previous episodes the authorities of The Village tried to beat Number

Number Six demonstrates his hypnotic powers.

Six on their own; this time they enlist The Villagers into the battle over Number Six's soul.

• Number Six is a fitness nut, jury-rigging a gymnasium in the woods and putting himself through demanding physical routines. It almost appears that he has successfully built a world of his own on the outskirts of The Village.

• Number Six makes no attempt to escape in this episode but instead is engaged in a favorite amusement—turning the tables on the authorities. It is interesting that Number Six takes advantage of the opportunities of mind-controlling drugs to influence a woman for his own cause.

• The tactics used by the authorities to control the minds of The Villagers are especially brutal in this episode—people strapped into chairs, isolated in rooms, pumped full of drugs, and at times lobotomized.

• It is easy to make comparisons between the committee in this episode and McCarthy's House Un-American Activities Committee of the 1950s. A common social good is established, and anyone outside the mainstream is subject to the whims of an angry lynch mob. "Unmutual," in this context, can be replaced with the political term "communist."

• The ethical ramifications of lobotomies were a hot topic in the late 1960s, and the practice was condemned in episodes like this one and such books as *One Flew Over the Cuckoo's Nest*. Lobotomies were most often performed on mental patients who exhibited antisocial, criminal behavior; the operations were conducted through the mid-1970s. A new form of the lobotomy is still practiced today, whereby lesions in the brain are medically transformed to curb aggressive behavior. And, indeed, drugs are still used in mental hospitals to curb "antisocial" behavior.

"HAMMER INTO ANVIL": EPISODE FOURTEEN

Writer: Roger Woddis
Script Editor: George Markstein
Producer: David Tomblin
Director: Pat Jackson
Executive Producer: Patrick McGoohan

CAST

Patrick McGoohan (Number Six), Patrick Cargill (Number Two), Victor Maddern (Band Master), Basil Hoskins (Number Fourteen), Norman Scace (Psychiatric Director), Derek Aylward (New Supervisor), Angelo Muscat (The Butler), Hilary Dwyer (Number Seventy-three), Arthur Gross (Control Room Operator), Peter Swanwick (Supervisor), Victor Woolf (Shop Assistant), Michael Segal (Laboratory Technician), Margo Andrew (Shop Kiosk Girl), Susan Sheers (Female Code Expert), Jackie Cooper (1st Guardian), Fred Haggerty (2nd Guardian), Eddie Powell (3rd Guardian), George Leach (4th Guardian).

CREW

Bernard Williams (Production Manager), Brendan J. Stafford (Director of Photography), Jack Shampan (Art Director), Jack Lowin (Camera Operator), Lee Doig (Editor), Ron Grainer (Musical Theme), Albert Elms (Musical Director), Robert Monks (2nd Unit Cameraman), Gino Marotta (Assistant Director), Ken Rolls (Sound Editor), John Bramall (Sound Recordist), Eric Mival (Music Editor), Rose Tobias-Shaw (Casting Director), Josie Fulford (Continuity), Kenneth Bridgeman (Set Dresser), Eddie Knight (Makeup), Pat McDermot (Hairdressing), Masada Wilmot (Wardrobe).

SYNOPSIS

A woman, Number Seventy-three, is being interrogated by Number Two. Bandages are wrapped around her wrists, which had been slashed earlier in a suicide attempt. Number Two, who doesn't look quite human, becomes especially brutal and sadistic during the interrogation. The woman screams. Number Six hears the screams from outside, rushes up the stairways and down the corridors to check out the situation. After wrestling past a couple of guards, he forces his way into the room. Number Two looks toward Number Six. Number Seventy-three, seeing her opportunity, jumps to her death outside the window. Number Two threatens Number Six, saying, "You'll pay for this." Number Six returns the threat, saying, "You will."

After a time, Number Six is forcibly brought to the offices of Number Two. Number Two threatens Number Six physically, pointing the tip of a sword at his eyes. He then threatens him intellectually, using a quote from Goethe about hammers and anvils: Number Two is theoretically the hammer, Number Six the anvil. Their confrontation is interrupted by a phone call to Number Two. The phone call, from superiors, will

Number Seventy-three is unable to withstand the torturous interrogation of Number Two.

reveal a weakness within Number Two: he is afraid of his masters. Number Six leaves, and Number Two orders special surveillance on Number Six.

Number Six begins a series of cryptic escapades designed to trouble Number Two. Knowing that he is being watched, he goes into a record store and listens to the same version of a song on six different records, all the time monitoring his watch. He leaves a copy of The Village newspaper with the word "security" circled and marked with a question mark. In his room he writes cryptic messages. Number Two intercepts one of these messages, which reads:

TO X.O.4 REF YOUR QUERY VIA BIZET RECORD. NO. 2'S INSTABILITY CONFIRMED. DETAILED REPORT FOLLOWS. D.6.

This message convinces Number Two that Number Six is a plant, placed by his superiors to report on him.

Number Six continues to feed Number Two's fears. He plants three blank pieces of paper in the cabin of a boat; Number Two finds them

Number Six promises to avenge the death of Number Seventy-three. Number Two isn't very concerned.

and desperately tries to decipher a message. Number Six places a cryptic, nonsensical ad in the personals of the local paper (actually a Spanish quote from *Don Quixote*). He calls The Village psychiatrist and asks about the "report" on Number Two. He makes special requests of The Village band. He has a birthday message from a dead person read over the loudspeakers to the people of The Village. All this confirms the paranoid thoughts of Number Two. He starts accusing his confidants of being in on the plan; he starts firing trusted employees. Number Six goes in for the kill. He sends off a cryptic message by homing pigeon. Number Two

Number Two is a defeated man at the end of the episode.

intercepts it, decodes it, and finds that it reads VITAL MESSAGE TO-
MORROW. 0600 HOURS BY VISUAL SIGNAL. At 0600 hours Number Six
goes to the beach and sends a signal in Morse code, using a mirror and
the sun.

Number Two finds himself completely isolated, trusting nobody.
Number Six decides to put an end to it all. He pays a visit to Number
Two, who is a shattered man, convinced that Number Six was planted
in The Village to spy on him. Number Six does nothing to alter this
thought. Instead he turns the tables: he charges Number Two with sabotage by interfering with Number Six's investigation. Number Two admits
defeat, pleads not to be reported. Number Six says he won't report him
but demands that Number Two report himself. Number Two picks up
the phone, calls his superiors, and says: "I have to report a breakdown
in control. Number Two needs to be replaced." Pleased, Number Six
leaves the offices.

OBSERVATIONS

- This episode begins with a challenge. After attempting to stop the
  torture of a woman by Number Two, Number Six is told: "You shouldn't
  have interfered, Number Six. You'll pay for it." Number Six replies:
  "You will." Again, the boundaries of the struggle have changed dramatically. Number Six is intent not on escape, but on a type of revenge.

- The tactics used by Number Six to battle Number Two are very much
  in the tradition of *Secret Agent*. In fact, we get a keen sense here of
  just how good Number Six must have been in his previous professional
  life. The relentless attack on Number Two is quite cerebral: like Iago
  in *Othello*, Number Six is able to plant the seeds of betrayal within
  Number Two's mind. Unlike Iago, however, Number Six has a reason
  to inflict this mental torture: he is righting a wrong.

- The truly absurd game kosho is played once again in this episode (it
  was played previously in "It's Your Funeral"). The script here sets the
  groundwork for the battle between Number Six and Number Two's
  faithful servant, Number Fourteen. It reads: "At first it appears to be a
  normal game, played hard but well within strict kosho rules. Then a
  new element creeps in. It becomes obvious that they are both playing
  for keeps. When the game has reached its deadliest point and we think
  we are going to see one or other of them killed, two new contestants
  appear. Number Fourteen and P (Number Six) have to break contact.
  They bow to each other in strict accordance with kosho ritual—but
  with a difference. As their heads go down their eyes remain level. They
  look at each other with mutual hatred."

- This episode pays several tributes to the classical arts, be it a quote
  from Goethe or Cervantes or a reference to the music of Bizet. We

have known all along that Number Six was a man of high culture. Perhaps here he is siding with some of the great heroes of the arts or—in the case of Don Quixote—a heroic fool.

• In the original script Number Six visits the grave of Number Seventy-three at the end of the episode. This was omitted from the final version. It may have put too much emphasis on Number Six's sympathies. But even with no final grave visit, it is becoming apparent that Number Six is taking on a role within this community. He is protecting the people from the abuses of society or at least enacting revenge against wrongs. This is most evident in episodes like "It's Your Funeral," in which he saves The Village from cruel and inevitable punishment.

"THE GIRL WHO WAS DEATH": EPISODE FIFTEEN

Writer: Terence Feely
From an idea by: David Tomblin
Producer: David Tomblin
Director: David Tomblin
Executive Producer: Patrick McGoohan

CAST

Patrick McGoohan (Number Six), Kenneth Griffith (Schnipps), Justine Lord (Sonia), Christopher Benjamin (Potter), Michael Brennan (Killer Karminski), Harold Berens (Boxing M.C.), Sheena Marsh (Barmaid), Max Faulkner (Scots Napoleon), John Rees (Welsh Napoleon), Joe Gladwin (Yorkshire Napoleon), John Drake (Bowler), Gaynor Steward (Little Girl), Graham Steward (1st Little Boy), Stephen How (2nd Little Boy).

CREW

Ronald Liles (Production Manager), Brendan J. Stafford (Director of Photography), Jack Shampan (Art Director), Len Harris (Camera Operator), Eric Boyd-Perkins (Editor), Albert Elms (Musical Director), Gino Marotta (Assistant Director), Wilfred Thompson (Sound Editor), Cyril Swern (Sound Recordist), Eric Mival (Music Editor), Rose Tobias-Shaw (Casting Director), John Lageu (Set Dresser), Phyllis Townshend (Continuity), Frank Turner (Makeup), Olive Mills (Hairdressing), Dora Lloyd (Wardrobe).

SYNOPSIS

A child's storybook comes to life. The story opens with a game of cricket, being played by some very proper-looking British gents. A ball is driven into the woods, and while a player tries to find it, a hand takes the ball and replaces it with another. This new ball is unwittingly used in the next round. This time, when the ball is put into action it explodes, killing a colonel named Hawke-Englishe.

Number Six learns from his colleague, Potter, that he is to carry on an investigation that Colonel Hawke-Englishe had started. A mad scientist named Schnipps is building a superrocket with the power to destroy London. The Colonel was working on it; now he's dead. Number Six readily accepts the assignment. As soon as he is on the case, Number Six finds himself involved in a crazy, tangled-up espionage game, being led from one location to another by a series of notes and messages. Each place he is led brings danger—explosions, violence. He's always making a close escape, only to find himself in another dangerous situation. At an amusement park he gets to know the enemy: she is a sporty, fashionable blonde named Sonia, and she appears to be enjoying her confrontations with Number Six.

Number Six follows Sonia in a sports car. After many winds and curves, she turns into the ghost village called Witchwood. Number Six loses sight of Sonia, then hears a female voice broadcast over loudspeakers. The voice says: "You may not see my face, but you may know my name. My name is Death." She then gives meaning to her name. In a series of incredible death devices, she puts Number Six to the test. Each test is more cunning than the one before, involving machine guns, trap doors ("Nice of you to drop in"), electrified spikes ("You'll get the

Number Six, disguised as Napoleon, is determined to save London from atomic attack.

point"), and exploding cyanide candles. Number Six escapes each perilous situation, to Sonia's delight. At the end, after Number Six has survived the ingenious tests, she reverts to simple militarism: pumping bombs out of a bazooka and, to her satisfaction, killing Number Six. But he isn't dead.

Sonia takes off from Witchwood in a helicopter. Number Six secretly hitches a ride, hanging from one of the bottom skis. The helicopter brings Sonia and Number Six to a lighthouse by the beach. Number Six infiltrates the lighthouse and, through a series of smart tricks, does away with the manned guards (who all look like Napoleon) one by one. Sonia (who we learn is the mad scientist Schnipps's daughter) eventually discovers Number Six and holds him at gunpoint. He is tied to a chair, placed in a room at the top of the lighthouse, and told about the plan. The entire lighthouse is a rocket. It is programmed to lift off from the beach and destroy London. Number Six is sitting in the nose cone, so he will be the first to visit the exploding city. Schnipps and Sonia say their good-byes and head out to gather a few belongings before setting out to sea.

Number Six unties the ropes and devises a plan to save London. After putting his plan into place, he jumps in the speedboat on the beach, takes off, and leaves Sonia and her father (who are still gathering a few last-minute items) in the lighthouse/rocket. There is a ticking noise. There is a smug look on Number Six's face. When Number Six is safe at sea, the entire lighthouse explodes, wiping out Sonia and Schnipps.

After the explosion, it becomes evident that the story is being told by Number Six to several children of The Village. He closes the storybook and says: "And that is how I saved London from the mad scientist." Number Two (looking like Schnipps), who has been observing this storytelling session with a woman (looking like Sonia), reacts with disgust. He thought Number Six might let down his guard with children and tell them something about why he resigned. Number Six looks toward the sleeping children and says: "Good night, children . . ." He then looks to the camera that is observing him and says, "Everywhere."

OBSERVATIONS

• This is an entertaining but lightweight episode, one that was actually written for *Secret Agent*. The script was revamped for *The Prisoner* late in the game, when the production team was running out of ideas for additional *Prisoner* episodes. It appears that the people involved had great fun reviving some old *Secret Agent* ideas. Christopher Benjamin, a regular on *Secret Agent*, plays the same role here: that of Potter. And there is a minor player in this episode, a bowler, who is played by an actor named John Drake.

• In an early scene Number Six thinks he's been poisoned. One of the big trivia questions surrounding the series concerns the names of the different drinks that Number Six consumes as an antidote to the poison. What were the drinks? In the appropriate order, they were brandy, whiskey, vodka, Drambuie, Tia Maria, Cointreau, and Grand Marnier. Don't try this at home, folks.

• If "Living in Harmony" was the most American of the episodes, "The Girl Who Was Death" is the most British. Number Six engages in a game of cricket, he goes to the pub for ale, and he engages in acts of pugilism. At the end, the Napoleon-like General has enlisted to his

Schnipps and his daughter Sonia have created the ultimate weapon.

WARNING
WHEN RED LIGHT
IS FLASHING
IT IS STRICTLY
FORBIDDEN
TO ENTER
UPPER CHAMBER

cause a motley crew that, together, represent various components of the British Commonwealth (Scots, Irish, Welsh).

• Although this episode appears somewhat contrived, it may actually be an indication of what the people behind *The Prisoner* were thinking about when they were charged with the creation of twenty-six episodes. It appears that ideas within The Village had been exhausted, and that there was a new but unsatisfactory emphasis on episodes, like this one, that were based outside The Village. If so, it shares a lot with "Do Not Forsake Me Oh My Darling" and "Living in Harmony," the last of which may have been dismissed as "un-*Prisoner*-like" if it hadn't run into so much controversy.

• The various guards in this episode are all dressed like Napoleon. In the original script they were to be dressed like "little Hitlers."

"ONCE UPON A TIME": EPISODE SIXTEEN

Writer: Patrick McGoohan
Script Editor: George Markstein
Producer: David Tomblin
Director: Patrick McGoohan
Executive Producer: Patrick McGoohan

CAST
Patrick McGoohan (Number Six), Leo McKern (Number Two), Angelo Muscat (The Butler), Peter Swanwick (Supervisor), John Cazabon (Umbrella Man).

CREW
Bernard Williams (Production Manager), Brendan J. Stafford (Director of Photography), Jack Shampan (Art Director), Jack Lowin (Camera Operator), Lee Doig (Editor), Ron Grainer (Musical Theme), Albert Elms (Incidental Music), Gino Marotta (Assistant Director), Wilfred Thompson (Sound Editor), John Bramall (Sound Recordist), Eric Mival (Music Editor), Rose Tobias-Shaw (Casting Director), Doris Martin (Continuity), Kenneth Bridgeman (Set Dresser), Eddie Knight (Makeup), Pat McDermot (Hairdressing), Masada Wilmot (Wardrobe).

SYNOPSIS
A familiar Number Two walks about his office. He tastes and then refuses breakfast. He's easily irritated, ordering The Butler around in a loud voice. He watches a pacing Number Six on the monitor, calls him, and asks: "Why do you care?" Number Six recognizes the voice (this Number Two had appeared in "The Chimes of Big Ben"), but he won't answer the question. Number Two watches as Number Six walks out of his dwelling and begins to intimidate a Villager. Everybody is on edge. Number Two thumbs through Number Six's file, and a series of flashbacks—documenting various forms of Number Six's revolt—are played out on the monitor. Eventually Number Two makes a phone call and demands approval for something called Degree Absolute. He claims to have no choice. After a fierce argument he is given approval. The test will last for seven days.

We learn throughout this episode that Degree Absolute is a dangerous method of interrogation based on psychoanalytic principles. It is a test of two individual wills. Only one of the individuals can survive the test. It is a desperate move by desperate men. At night Number Six is prepared for the test: he is put under a type of electronic hypnosis and grilled continuously by The Supervisor. In the morning Degree Absolute begins.

Number Two wakes Number Six from sleep and introduces him to the room in which the experiments will take place. Number Six has reverted to a childlike state, licking an ice-cream cone and spewing nursery rhymes. Number Two recites a Shakespearean passage about the "seven stages of man." This is the first stage: "the infant, mewling and puking in the nurse's arms." During each progressive stage, Number Two grills Number Six about his feelings, his motives, his surroundings, and his situations—always trying to catch him off guard, to get an answer to the big question: "Why did you resign?" In every situation Number Two plays the authority figure. At first he's the father; Number Six is the son. Other role-playing relationships will continue through the experiments,

Number Six plays out the first stages of Degree Absolute.

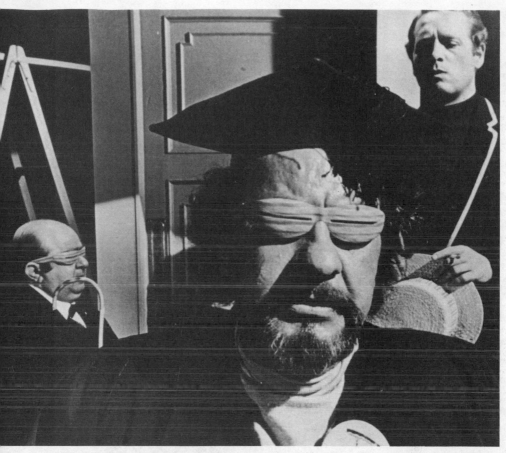

Number Two assumes the role of teacher while Number Six assumes the role of student, hat in hand.

including teacher/student; coach/athlete; employer/employee; judge/accused; officer/soldier; and, finally, prison guard/prisoner. During each stage, the grilling becomes more intense and the questions more to the point. At every sign of weakness, Number Two asks why he resigned. Number Six successfully rebels. The struggle becomes physical, wearing both men down.

Number Six regains consciousness, and he is impressed by the ingenuity of Degree Absolute. He comes to understand the subtleties and to recognize the very real risk Number Two is running. He discovers that he is in the embryo room, and that neither he nor Number Two can leave the room until the experiment is over—until one of them breaks. The experiments continue. The two men drink together; laugh together; intimidate each other. Then the final minutes begin. Number Six locks Number Two behind the bars of a real prison; Number Six is gaining an edge. As if to accent the turn of events, The Butler begins taking his

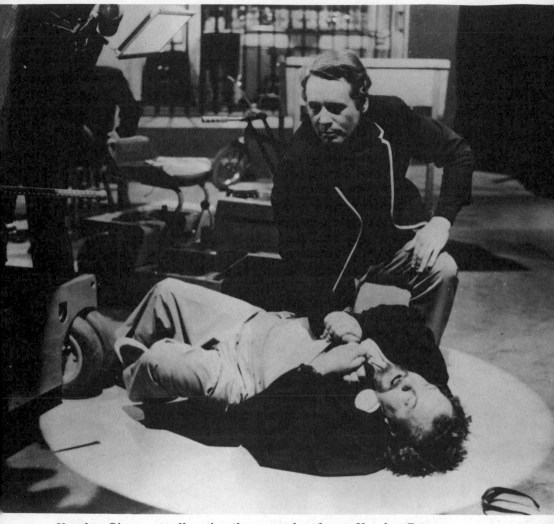

Number Six eventually gains the upper hand over Number Two.

orders from Number Six. When only three minutes remain, Number Six turns the tables and begins a ruthless interrogation of Number Two. With two minutes left he opens the door and starts counting off the seconds. Within the final seconds Number Six stops counting numbers and instead chants: "Die, die, die, die, die."

Number Two collapses at the last second. Number Six checks his pulse; finds him dead. The Supervisor enters the room and congratulates Number Six. Number Six throws down a glass, as if disturbed by what has just transpired. The Supervisor asks what it is that Number Six desires. Number Six says only: "Number One." The Supervisor says, "I'll take you." He leads Number Six into a corridor, the doors close tight behind them, and Number Two lies very dead in his prison cell.

OBSERVATIONS

- One of the cruelest juxtapositions in the history of television was to broadcast "The Girl Who Was Death," a sweet nothing of a tale, one week before this: the most baffling, the most revealing, and the most brilliant of all *Prisoner* episodes. It is especially important to note that this episode was written *and* directed by Patrick McGoohan.

- This was originally conceived as the final episode in the first group of thirteen. It is hard to think about this episode without thinking about the final episode, "Fall Out," as well. However, "Fall Out" was not even in the planning stages at the time this was filmed.

    The exact amount of time that elapsed between "Once Upon a Time" and "Fall Out" is open to some question, but it could be as long as six months. When it was decided that *The Prisoner* would last only seventeen episodes, "Once Upon a Time" was designated as the "penultimate" episode and shelved. It was decided that something would follow it. That something was "Fall Out."

- The ultimate method used in "Once Upon a Time" to break Number Six, Degree Absolute, is based entirely on psychological principles. It is also performed one on one. McGoohan would probably consider this a fair fight—and a fight his character, Number Six, could win.

- In this episode Number Six gives the most direct answer to the question "Why did you resign?" After intense interrogation, he says simply, "I resigned for peace of mind."

- This episode answers one question that most viewers probably weren't asking. The original end credits for *The Prisoner* series were quite different from what appeared in the broadcast series. In the original version, after the credits have appeared, the penny-farthing wheels start to turn into globes of the Earth and universe, which then are covered up by three letters that fill the entire screen: POP. In the final version this sequence was replaced by images of Rover scooting across the water. Originally, the word "POP" was probably conceived as another mystery, one that is explained in "Once Upon a Time."

    POP is an acronym for "protect other people." It's a noble thought, one that Number Six lives by in multiple episodes (especially with damsels in distress or, more courageously, in "It's Your Funeral"). But it also has military connotations. The society's desire to protect people can result in a big bang (or POP). This gives more credence to those who interpret *The Prisoner* as some type of apocalyptic tale about nuclear destruction. But its message is lost (or at least obscured) by the fact that the big mystery POP didn't appear in the previous episodes. If you would like to see the original ending, it is included in "The Alternate Chimes of Big Ben," available on videocassette.

• Patrick McGoohan reportedly wrote the script to this episode in a thirty-six hour period.

"FALL OUT": EPISODE SEVENTEEN

Writer: Patrick McGoohan
Producer: David Tomblin
Director: Patrick McGoohan
Executive Producer: Patrick McGoohan

CAST

Patrick McGoohan (Number Six), Leo McKern (Number Two), Alexis Kanner (Number Forty-eight), Kenneth Griffith (The President), Angelo Muscat (The Butler), Peter Swanwick (The Supervisor), Michael Miller (The Delegate).

CREW

Ronald Liles (Production Manager), Brendan J. Stafford (Director of Photography), Jack Shampan (Art Director), Len Harris, Bob Kindred (Camera Operators), Noreen Ackland, Eric Boyd-Perkins (Editors), Ron Grainer (Musical Theme), Albert Elms (Musical Director), Gino Marotta (Assistant Director), Wilfred Thompson (Sound Editor), Cyril Swern (Sound Recordist), Eric Mival (Music Editor), Rose Tobias Shaw (Casting Director), John Lageu (Set Dresser), Phyllis Townshend (Continuity), Frank Turner (Makeup), Olive Mills (Hairdressing), Dora Lloyd (Wardrobe).

SYNOPSIS

The episode begins with flashback sequences from "Once Upon a Time." Highlights document the prior episode, and then it carries on from where it left off, with Number Six being led through various underground corridors and mazes in search of Number One. Each door brings him closer to the heart of power. One door is opened, and he sees a sculpture of himself in a coatroom. Another door is opened, and it is lined with jukeboxes that play the Beatles' "All You Need Is Love." Finally a door is opened to a chamber filled mostly with masked people, who are seated as if in a jury and are identified by type (Defectors, Activists, Reactionaries, Nationalists, Pacifists, and so on).

The President, donning a whig like a British judge, welcomes Number Six and addresses the session. He announces that the community is in a state of democratic crisis. The President understands that Number Six has survived the ultimate test, and he says that the man standing before him should no longer be referred to as Number Six or as any number: "He has gloriously vindicated the right of the individual to be individual." He is now addressed as "Sir."

The President states that a transfer of ultimate power is under way.

He invites Number Six to watch the "tedious" ceremonies. Number Six watches, seated on a throne. First off, The President orders the resuscitation of Number Two, who had died in the previous episode. Several men take Number Two, place him on stretcher, lather his face, and put a strange machine on his head. The President then begins to discuss the three forms of revolt.

The first is the revolt of youth, and Number Forty-eight is brought before the session as an example of youth's rebellion. He is charged with revolt. Number Forty-eight, who speaks in a 1960s slang, starts breaking out in song, singing, "Collarbone's connected to the neckbone. Neckbone's connected to the headbone. Now hear the word of the Lord."

The President invites Number Six to "lead us or go."

He causes general havoc in the assembly and refuses to sit still. Number Forty-eight is found guilty of revolt, but his sentence is delayed until Number Six's inauguration. He is forced to exit the room.

The second man accused of revolt is Number Two from "Once Upon a Time"—a man who has been brought back from the dead. On waking, he says, "I feel a new man!" He begins to speak boisterously, causing trouble. Throwing caution to the wind, he even spits in the mechanical eye of what may be Number One. He is found guilty of being a successful, secure member of the establishment who bites the hand that feeds him. This is the second form of revolt. Like Number Forty-eight, his sentencing will be delayed. He is banished from the room.

Number Forty-eight is found guilty of youthful rebellion.

Finally, the pure revolt of Number Six (who sits smugly on the throne) is not condemned but, instead, saluted. The President says: "We are honored to have with us a revolutionary of a different caliber. He has revolted. Resisted. Fought. Held fast. Maintained. Destroyed resistance. Overcome coercion. The right to be a Person, Someone, or Individual. We applaud his private war and concede that despite materialistic efforts he has survived intact and secure. All that remains is recognition of a Man." After making this stirring speech, The President offers Number Six a choice: "to lead us or go." To make it perfectly clear that Number

Number Two is found guilty of "biting the hand that feeds him."

Six has the option to be free, he is given a key to his home in London, a million in traveler's checks, and a passport. Number Six is not sure whether he wants to lead or go. He is invited to address the assembly and accepts willingly. But when he tries to speak his mind, he is shouted down by members of the assembly (every time he begins his speech with "I," they shout, "Aye, aye, aye, aye, aye . . ."). Number Six is shaken by this reaction. The President thanks him for the speech and invites him to meet Number One.

Number Six is led down many guarded corridors, going deeper and deeper underground. On the way he sees Number Forty-eight and Number Two in transparent capsules that read "Orbit 48" and "Orbit 2." Number Six climbs a circular staircase, pushes a button, and is allowed to enter a room full of globes. At the end of this room sits a hooded figure, its back to Number Six. The figure stands, turns toward Number

Number Six represents the pure form of revolt, and is encouraged to address the members of the chamber.

Six, and offers him a crystal ball. Number Six drops the ball, reaches for the mask, and pulls it off. Underneath is the mask of a chattering chimpanzee. Number Six pulls off this mask. Underneath is Number Six himself, looking evil and threatening. Number Six chases this image of himself out of the room and locks him out.

Suddenly havoc breaks loose. Chaos reigns. Number Six enlists The Butler, Number Forty-eight, and Number Two to help him overcome the authorities. They surprise hooded figures with a fire extinguisher, steal their clothing, and confront several armed guards. They take the guards' guns and enter the main room, ready to fight. The bullets are fired fast and furious. The four conspirators realize that they are inside a rocket ship, and Number Six sets the gears in motion for the ship to launch. Outside, The Villagers are being evacuated. Inside, a tense countdown proceeds, and the rocket slowly but forcefully takes off. The President sends helicopters out to intercept the rocket, but this escape is real and inevitable.

Number Six, Number Two, and Number Forty-eight are suddenly on the A20 Freeway, twenty-seven miles outside of London. They ride in the back of a truck (which is actually the prison set from "Once Upon a Time"). They dance happily while the song "Dem Bones" plays on a passing car radio. On the highway, the truck stops and Number Forty-eight is released. He hitchhikes down the road, free. Driving the truck is The Butler. He is forced to stop the truck in the heart of London, when a policeman pulls them over. Number Two walks almost as if he were directed to the House of Lords. Number Six and The Butler hop on a double-decker bus and arrive at 1 Buckingham Place, the London home of Number Six. The Butler walks up to the door. It opens by itself, and The Butler walks in. Number Six gets in his Lotus 7 and hits the highway. The words "The Prisoner" are superimposed over the screen as Number Six drives away. The car then starts driving as it did in the opening credit sequences.

OBSERVATIONS

• This is the episode where mysteries are supposed to be solved, and at least one mystery is solved during the first few moments. Almost immediately we learn where this series was filmed. Until this episode it had been a highly guarded secret. Here, the opening credits read: "The Prisoner. In the grounds of The Hotel Portmeirion, Penrhyndeudraeth, North Wales, by courtesy of Mr. Clough Williams-Ellis." We learn—in one sense, at least—that The Village is a very real place; it is not some kind of studio set. Clough Williams-Ellis was the architect of the resort, and—while he was happy to make this location available—he did it on condition that no publicity be given out while the series was being filmed. (It has also been reported that Williams-Ellis would often follow behind various personnel, cleaning up after them.)

Every year, the Six of One Club holds a *Prisoner* convention at Portmeirion. Information on the convention is detailed in the appendix, under "Sources of Information."

• This is actually the second part of the final episode, the first of which is "Once Upon a Time." Because of the various characters and situations that are cross-referenced between the episodes, they cannot be watched—or understood—independently of one another.

While the two episodes are interdependent, they couldn't be more different from one another. "Once Upon a Time" is a minimalist psychological drama. Its success depends solely on strong performances by two individuals, Patrick McGoohan and Leo McKern. "Fall Out" is a colorful, sprawling display of ideas, with a cast of at least fifty performers and extras. Both episodes are exhausting, but for very different reasons.

• In the original script McGoohan had the opening jukeboxes blaring forth a "wailing cacophony" of sound. The songs he noted for possible use in this sequence included "All You Need Is Love," "Little Boxes," "Toot-Toot-Tootsie Goodbye," "Hello, Dolly," and "Yellow Submarine." It has been noted that they actually tried this scene with numerous songs, but it sounded like a mess. The decision was eventually made to use only one song, and that was "All You Need Is Love."

The choice of the Beatles' song was fortunate, for it doesn't really date the episode. *The Prisoner* and the Beatles remain popular in their own rights these days; they haven't yet been relegated to pure nostalgia (and perhaps they never will be). But what can be read into this song? Why was it chosen for this episode?

The song plays ironically, no doubt—especially at the end, when the guns are going off. But it also identifies something wrong with The Village. At times, during the various episodes, a character is introduced who shows emotion—but seldom, if ever, love. Except for the London scene with Janet in "Do Not Forsake Me Oh My Darling," the only love in the series is either induced (as in "Checkmate") or abused (as the love between The Professor and his wife in "The General"). Number Six certainly never falls in love. Some, posing questions in this episode, have found answers in this choice of song. It has been argued that a simple solution to The Village's (and, allegorically, society's) problems is staring us in the face: all we need is love.

• McGoohan has stated that "if there are any answers to *The Prisoner*, they are in the final episode." It is difficult to find any clear-cut answers to questions such as "Who is Number One?" or "Why did The Prisoner resign?" But there *are* solid answers to the question of why this series was made. For one thing, *The Prisoner* is about revolt, and the viewer is offered a type of sermon on revolt. According to this episode, there are three very different types of revolt: 1) the rebellion of youth, which is usually rebelling against nothing in particular; 2) the rebellion of members of the establishment, who "bite the hand that feeds them"; and 3) the pure revolt of an individual against the whims and constraints

Leo McKern had trimmed his hair and shaved his beard between the filming of "Once Upon a Time" and "Fall Out." A special barbering scene was added to address the inconsistency.

of society. Number Six, of course, represents the third, pure form of revolt—the only form that makes a difference.

- Months went by between the filming of "Once Upon a Time" and "Fall Out." During that lapse, Leo McKern trimmed his hair and shaved his beard (and went on with his life). When he was asked to replay his role as Number Two in "Fall Out," he refused to grow back the beard and the hair. Thus, continuity demanded that a special scene be added in which the beard was shaved and the hair trimmed. It is for this, and for no other reason, that Number Two in "Fall Out" is a reasonably clean-cut fellow (he still sports a mustache).

- A real estate sign is seen in front of Number Six's London home during this episode. The name of the real estate company is Lageu & Son, Estate Agents. This is something of an in-joke; John Lageu was employed during this episode as the set dresser.

- Number Two asks some interesting questions in this episode, especially concerning his own death. While watching his death on a monitor, he asks, "How did you do it?" and speculates that perhaps it was something in the wineglass. Are we to suspect that the authorities had something to do with his death? We know that they are very willing to kill off their chief commanders, but we'd have to struggle to find some reason for them to kill Number Two—the one man who was willing to risk his life to get information from Number Six. The only plausible reason is that Number Two is found guilty of insubordination. He forced the issue of Degree Absolute, perhaps against the directives of the authorities.

    On closer examination, it appears that Number Two was always aware that his death was imminent if he failed. When introducing a childlike Number Six to the Degree Absolute concept, he writes three objectives on the board: 1. Find Missing Link; 2. Put It Together; and 3. (If he fails) Bang!

CHAPTER TWO

NOTES, ANECDOTES, AND NONSENSE

There have been plenty of stories told about *The Prisoner* for the past twenty years, and we've collected some of the best of them for this chapter. Although we've tried hard to verify the accuracy of these notes and anecdotes, some of them must be relegated to the slush pile of rumor and hearsay. The research gets especially problematic concerning the contradictory recollections of certain individuals involved in the making of *The Prisoner*.

Like statements in the *Tally Ho* itself, you can't always believe what you read. Every once in a while someone will print that Ian Fleming, the creator of James Bond, appears in "The General." As Bruce Clark, American coordinator of the Six of One Club, has pointed out, Ian Fleming died two years before *The Prisoner* was put into production. So it goes. We've tried to eliminate any such faux pas, but perhaps something slipped by. If so, let us know about it.

MOONLIGHTING

The Prisoner originally aired in the United States as a summer replacement for *The Jackie Gleason Show*.

THE NUMBER SIX

In numerology, the number six represents ambivalence and equilibrium. Could this be why McGoohan chose this particular number for the central character? If so, he's not saying. McGoohan claims that the number six was chosen because it is the only number that, when turned upside down, is something else.

THE BIRTH OF *THE PRISONER*

Secret Agent had become such a popular television series during the mid-1960s that ITC—the production company in Great Britain—commissioned hour-long color episodes for the 1966–67 season. After two episodes of the new *Secret Agent* were shot, McGoohan walked into the offices of Lew Grade (the chief executive at ITC) and said: "I want a change. I've got this thing with me. ..."

"This thing" in McGoohan's briefcase was actually notes and diagrams (and possibly at least one script) for a miniseries to be called *The Prisoner*. Lew Grade could very well have challenged McGoohan to give up on the idea or at least delay it until the 1966–67 season of *Secret Agent* was shot and in the can (after all, *Secret Agent* was one of the most successful television shows in ITC's history). Instead, after reviewing the materials, Grade reportedly said: "You know it's so crazy, it might work. When can you start?"

McGoohan started immediately, taking most of the crew from *Secret Agent* with him. The two color episodes shot for *Secret Agent* were not discarded, however. Although the series officially ended, these two episodes were combined in the made-for-TV movie *Koroshi* (now on videocassette).

TAKE SEVEN! . . . TAKE TWENTY-SIX (OR THIRTY)! . . . TAKE SEVENTEEN! . . .

As discussed above, the way the story has traditionally been told is that Patrick McGoohan had been working on *The Prisoner* while performing his duties as John Drake in *Secret Agent* (*Danger Man* in the U.K.). Originally McGoohan introduced the concept of *The Prisoner* as a seven-episode miniseries. Lew Grade was intrigued with the idea, but he couldn't commit to the miniseries concept that McGoohan had in mind. According to Grade, twenty-six episodes would have to be produced in order to make it a feasible and profitable idea. McGoohan was persuaded to expand the concept, although he maintains that "I only wanted to do seven. ... Out of all the scripts there are seven that I would pick and put in line, and I'd just keep those and throw the rest away."

The production was scheduled in two prolonged sessions, each of which would produce thirteen episodes. After the first thirteen were completed, it became apparent that the idea was running out of steam. ITC and McGoohan agreed to press on with four more episodes and then end the series. This created its own problems—much of the crew (and McGoohan himself) had made commitments during the break period that was originally scheduled between the two sessions. To complete the final four episodes, it was necessary to enlist almost an entirely new crew. The final episodes were shot by mostly new people, and then the series was put to bed.

For the past couple of years this version of events has been falling apart, bit by bit. First of all it appears that McGoohan had material in his hands for five or six script ideas (not seven as originally reported). It also appears that Lew Grade had commissioned not twenty-six but thirty episodes, in keeping with standard syndication practices of the day. It also has been noted that the series was cut short not because it ran out of ideas, but because it was taking too much money and too much time. After two years in production, ITC pulled the plug.

Finally, it seems the "production break" that was set between the thirteen episodes may have been a fabrication. The reason for the change of crew members after thirteen episodes has more to do with personality

Nadia as she appeared in "Chimes of Big Ben," one of the "original" seven episodes.

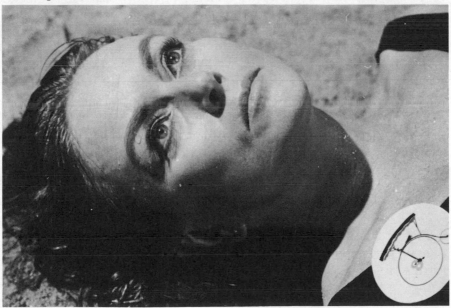

problems than with "production breaks" and "prior commitments." After an argument with McGoohan, George Markstein (the script editor) quit the show. This happened after production of the thirteenth episode. Several production personnel followed him out the door.

It seems we have a softened "official" version of events and a more nasty "real" version. The truth may lie somewhere in between. Its importance to the enjoyment of *The Prisoner* is questionable, but there is some natural curiosity about the unusual number of episodes (seventeen) and the abrupt change in personnel. And most *Prisoner* fans feel entitled to some behind-the-scenes gossip, no matter whether that gossip can be authenticated or made straight with the different tellers. We do know one thing for sure, however, and that's the names of the seven episodes that McGoohan says "really count." They are (in McGoohan's order):

1. "Arrival"
2. "Free for All"
3. "Dance of the Dead"
4. "Checkmate"
5. "The Chimes of Big Ben"
6. "Once Upon a Time"
7. Conclusion ("Fall Out")

THE PENNY-FARTHING BICYCLE

The ubiquitous penny-farthing bicycle was displayed on personnel badges, on helicopters, on canned goods, on taxis, on The Village flag—indeed, it is the most dominant and most misunderstood symbol in *The Prisoner*. Patrick McGoohan, on discussing the meaning of the penny-farthing, has said: "I came up with the penny-farthing bicycle because I thought it was an ironic symbol of progress. The feeling is that we are going too fast. . . . I wish we could go a bit slower, but we can't."

LOCATION

In "The Chimes of Big Ben," The Village is said to be in "Lithuania, on the Baltic, thirty miles from the Polish border." In "Many Happy Returns," The Village is thought to be an island off the coast of Morocco. In "Fall Out," The Village appears to be at the end of a tunnel leading to the A20 in Kent.

GO FOR HELP

In 1982 Rockumentary Films made a music video for the song "I Helped Patrick McGoohan Escape." This song, performed by the Times, features scenes of Portmeirion and other *Prisoner* locations.

NOT 6, BUT 007

Patrick McGoohan was the first choice to play the supercool character James Bond in the movies. McGoohan turned down the role (and considerable riches) twice. In fact, it was McGoohan who, after turning down the role of James Bond, first suggested Sean Connery. When Connery quit the character, McGoohan was again offered the role. Again he declined. The role went to George Lazenby (and later, of course, to Roger Moore).

Even the food canisters at the "general stores" are adorned with the ubiquitous pennyfarthing symbol.

Determining the exact location of The Village is a favorite activity of *Prisoner* fans.

BRAVO!

Ron Grainer composed the exceptional theme music to *The Prisoner*. His other television credits include theme music for *Dr. Who* and *Tales of the Unexpected*. Grainer died in 1981.

WHO WAS THAT MAN?

George Markstein, a former reporter on British intelligence matters during World War II, was the script editor for *The Prisoner*. He appears at the beginning of every episode except "Fall Out." He is the man behind the desk during the opening credits, when Number Six turns in his resignation. Markstein and McGoohan had a falling-out over the series. After thirteen episodes were shot, Markstein quit the program.

EVERYMAN FOR HIMSELF

The name of McGoohan's production company is Everyman Films, Ltd. Although it hasn't been substantiated by McGoohan, it is often thought to be a side reference to the medieval morality play *Everyman*, which is an allegorical study of mankind.

PREAMBLE

Before Patrick McGoohan took up acting, he worked in a steel mill, in a bank, and as a chicken farmer.

PLAY FOR PAY

The "extras" used in the chess game during "Checkmate" were paid two pounds ten shillings (around $5 U.S. dollars) for each of their performances. Perhaps these meager wages help explain why it was difficult to get all the "chess pieces" to move properly.

It was very difficult to get the "extras" to move properly during the human game of chess in "Checkmate."

THE QUEST FOR MEANING

Angelo Muscat, who portrays The Butler, appears in *every* episode. He is the only character other than Number Six to do so. What meaning can we attribute to this? ITC published a small "press information" booklet to address this and other questions. About The Butler, they wrote, "He is the little man of every community, prepared to follow faithfully, like sheep, any established order." Maybe there's something here, but it

Angelo Muscat, who portrays The Butler, is the only character other than Number Six to appear in every episode.

appears that the production company felt it necessary to answer in advance the questions they knew would be asked. Here are some of their official answers to other controversial questions (we suggest you sprinkle a good deal of salt over the answers):

Q: What does The Village represent?

A: The Village could be the real and unconscious world of civilization today. We are all prisoners without bars.

Q. What do the numbers—Number 6, Number 2, and so on—symbolize?

A: We live in a dehumanizing society, where the individuality of man is being submerged, and the computerization of man has taken over.

Q: The ever-present eye? Is the world and its people being watched just like the inhabitants of The Village?

A: Not yet. Not completely. Not everyone. But the danger is omnipresent.

Q: Is there no trust in The Village?

A: What has happened to trust among nations?

Q: Can science interpose into an individual's dreams?

A: Number Six says no. This spirit of the individual is supreme. The possibility is haunting, though. How many Number Sixes are there in the world?

Q: Is the whole world a flim-flam for "happiness"?

A: To all the inhabitants of The Village it is. Answer for yourself the compromises you make for "happiness."

Q: Kid me not. Votes are important. Democracy is not a sham. What are McGoohan's beliefs?

A: We do not query McGoohan, but in The Village elections are a platitudinous sham, full of empty, cynical promises.

Q: Where is passion, love, kisses, in The Village?

A: In the Village there are pleasantries, the only level of passion automatons are capable of.

Q: What happens to fun at The Village?

A: There is plenty of fun at The Village, all manufactured.

Q: Is there anything in existence like the balloon—Rover?

A: Only in the mind's eye.

Q: What is the meaning of Rover?

A: Rover symbolizes repression and the guardianship of corrupt authority, which, when corruption is finally overcome, disintegrates.

Q: Does Number Six finally become Number One? Is this the be-all and end-all of his rebellion?

The balloon-like Rover continues to be among the most puzzling and powerful characters developed for a television show.

A: In the last episode, "Fall Out," he assumes the seat of Number One, only to give it up voluntarily. The Prisoner may have a yen to be the warden, but in his saner moments he would rather not live in a prison environment.

Q: What is the meaning of the "shouting down" of McGoohan by the hooded assembly in the last episode?

A: The inability of the ordinary man to make his voice heard—to put forward his viewpoint to the world.

Q: What about the theme of "love, love, love" in the last episode, amidst all that terror?

A: This is a protest against the paradoxes that exist in modern civilization. Man preaching love, love, love while wars and hate persist.

Q: Who is really that charming "hippy" character?

Alexis Kanner (with the top hat) had major roles in "Living in Harmony" and in "Fall Out." He also has a short, uncredited appearance in "The Girl Who Was Death."

A: He symbolizes youth in rebellion against the Establishment. The young man is seen trying to thumb a lift first in one direction and then in another on a highway. He represents youth not knowing or caring in which direction it goes.

Q: What about the penny-farthing symbol?

A: That represents the slowness of progress in our modern civilization.

AN OLD DOG, SOME NEW TRICKS

David Tomblin, McGoohan's chief collaborator on the series, went on to assist Steven Spielberg in the direction of *Raiders of the Lost Ark*.

WELCOME TO THE VILLAGE

The Village is actually a resort in Portmeirion on Cardigan Bay in North Wales. Conceived by the brilliant architect Sir Clough Williams-Ellis, it has been a favorite refuge for such notable writers as Bertrand Russell, George Bernard Shaw, and Noel Coward. Patrick McGoohan first became acquainted with the resort in 1959, when it was used as a location site for *Danger Man*.

THE X IS IN

In the opening sequence of *The Prisoner*, a photo of Number Six is defaced by a series of x's typed over it. The photo of McGoohan was not specifically created for *The Prisoner*. It is McGoohan's official publicity portrait, and it is also shown on placards in the episode "Free for All" and as proof of identity in "Do Not Forsake Me Oh My Darling." It may be McGoohan's subtle way of striking out at the publicity process, a process that he—as one of the most popular actors in the world—knew much about. It has also been interpreted as a link to his former role, John Drake in *Secret Agent*. According to this insight, John Drake is being x-ed out, and Number Six is taking form.

THE EYE IN THE SKY

The bald-headed Village Supervisor, played by Peter Swanwick, appears in nine episodes. The only characters to appear in more episodes are Number Six and The Butler.

WHAT'S IN A NAME?

Several episodes underwent last-minute name changes. "Once Upon a Time" was originally entitled "Degree Absolute." "Checkmate" was produced under the name "The Queen's Pawn." "A. B. and C." had gone

Number Six's car is a Lotus 7, a model that was discontinued in 1982.

under two different names: "Play in Three Acts" and "1, 2, and 3." "Do Not Forsake Me Oh My Darling" was originally entitled "Face Unknown."

BASED ON FACT

Patrick McGoohan has stated more than once that *The Prisoner* was based on fact, that there was indeed an espionage internment camp similar to The Village. The most striking possibility for a factual basis concerns the organization known as the Inter-Services Research Bureau (ISRB). During World War II, the ISRB sent certain people to a location in Scotland for "holidays." These people had valuable knowledge of one sort or another, and the state wanted to ensure that the knowledge remained secret and confidential. Although they were extremely well-treated in this luxury camp, they were not allowed to leave.

George Markstein, the script editor for *The Prisoner*, learned about such prisons as a journalist during World War II. He reported frequently on intelligence matters and eventually wrote a fictitious account of a villagelike place. Today the belief persists that both Eastern and Western regimes have created special prisons for those possessing sensitive secrets of state. Be seeing you!

KAR 120C

The numbers above appear on the license plate of Number Six's car. The famous car is a Lotus 7, a model introduced in 1957 and discontinued in 1982. Two different Lotus 7's appear in *The Prisoner*. The first was sold off when it was thought that all scenes involving the car were completed. A second one had to be purchased when a script again called for the car.

HEAVY METAL

In Iron Maiden's heavy metal album *Power Slave*, there is a track entitled "Back in the Village." The song ends with the lyrics "I don't have a number, I'm a name." Iron Maiden paid tribute to *The Prisoner* more directly in an album called *The Number of the Beast*: a song entitled "The Prisoner" begins with the opening sound track of the television series.

BE SEEING YOU

In several episodes characters in The Village sign off with a special hand signal something like a salute, after saying, "Be seeing you." According to Norma West—the actress who portrayed the observer in "Dance of the Dead"—Patrick McGoohan explained the meaning of the salute to her during production. It is the same signal that was once used by the ancient Christians: the sign of the fish.

WHAT'S MISSING?

The opening episode of the series, "Arrival," originally ran for one and a half hours. Geoffrey Foot, the editor, was responsible for cutting it down to a more manageable fifty-six minutes.

HALF A DOZEN

The interior scenes in *The Prisoner* were shot not at Portmeirion, but at an MGM studio lot in London. The set used for *The Prisoner* was actually built for *The Dirty Dozen*. Many scenes at the French village in *The Dirty Dozen* are recognizable as *Prisoner* locations.

LOGOS

Most movie and television logos are created from scratch: artists are contracted to create a logo that represents the idea of the show. Not so for *The Prisoner*. The logo and all graphics that appear in the series were set in a typeface called Albertus, designed in the 1930s by Berthold Wolp. A few minor alterations were made (most notably opening up the "e"). If you want to reproduce the typeface, it is available in art shops through Letraset press-type.

RED ROVER, WHITE ROVER . . .

Rover, the buoyant weather balloon that facelessly enforces The Village's laws, is perhaps the most bizarre character in television history. Originally this ominous police vehicle was conceived as a faceless, driverless Volkswagen with a blue light on top. Such a vehicle was actually created for *The Prisoner*, but it failed one major test: when placed in the ocean during a critical point of preproduction, it quickly filled with water and sank. Unable to retrieve this vehicle, McGoohan looked to the skies for assistance and found it in a passing weather balloon. McGoohan asked his production manager, Bernard Williams, to inquire as to the availability of such a balloon. "He took off like a rocket, and after we had done a few shots, he arrived back with a station wagon full of these balloons in varying sizes, from six inches up to eight feet in diameter, as well as cylinders of oxygen and helium and various other things. That's how we got what turned out to be the best-possible menacing Rover that one could have." Rover remains the show's most expensive special effect.

(Some people are starting to question this story, which has been told for years. No production photos exist showing the Volkswagen contraption. And it has been documented that when the crew first arrived on location at Portmeirion, they had weather balloons in their possession.

The balloon-like Rover was the most expensive special effect in *The Prisoner*.

However, the early scripts all make reference to a machine-driven Rover with a light on top.)

ALTERNATE CHIMES

An alternate version of the landmark episode "The Chimes of Big Ben" has recently been discovered, and it's raised questions as to whether other alternate episodes exist. Early in 1967, the original version of "The Chimes of Big Ben" was completed as a press preview. Before the series aired, however, this episode was taken back to the editing room for dozens of last-minute changes. The original version never aired in the U.K., nor was it shown on CBS during the screenings. Rumors of its existence set off an international search by The Prisoner Appreciation Society. A year of searching turned up a 16-mm print in a Toronto, Canada, film vault. Scheduled to be destroyed along with other films that had been replaced by videotape, it was instead delivered to The Prisoner Appreciation Society for verification and study. Over two dozen differences have been documented, the most significant of which (beyond theme music and dialogue) are:

- A very different opening sequence, with a different musical score.
- Number Six using an ancient Greek triquetrum to geographically locate The Village.
- A closing credit explanation of the symbolic penny-farthing bicycle.

THE L.A. TAPES

The recent discovery of an alternate version of "The Chimes of Big Ben" gives hope to the discovery and eventual release of some intriguing "lost" *Prisoner* materials. The most controversial concerns a one-hour-long interview with Patrick McGoohan that was followed by a six-minute "piece of fun." The interview, coordinated by McGoohan himself with his daughter asking the questions, has never been shown commercially—injunctions were threatened by several persons concerning the release of the film. Generally designated as "The L.A. Tapes," the only known copy is in the vaults of the British television concern Channel 4. The interview reportedly features McGoohan discussing James Bond, *The Prisoner* crew, and the identity of Number One. The six-minute "piece of fun" is an allegorical *Prisoner*-oriented film that employs coat hangers as a recurrent symbol (why coat hangers? As one *Prisoner* fan has speculated, a coat hanger is simply a question mark with a bar underneath). During the interview McGoohan claims that he has edited down the seventeen-episode series into a four-hour movie, and that he is working on another film, called *Stop*, which borrows heavily from the ideas of *The Prisoner*.

THOUGHT YOU'D LIKE TO KNOW

In 1985 the United States government classified 19,607,736 documents as "secret."

WORKING TITLE: *THE PRISONER*

Before the first script was written, Patrick McGoohan and his cohorts George Markstein and David Tomblin prepared various materials to generate excitement about the idea of *The Prisoner* and to brief potential screenwriters and other participants about the nuances of the series. One of the few remaining early documents is a four-page paper created by script editor George Markstein that was intended to provide a brief overview of *The Prisoner*. It has no title. At the top of the paper are the following words:

T.V. Series—Working Title—
"The Prisoner"

The paper is printed here in full. There are many intriguing ideas that were never incorporated into the actual series, the most fanciful being the Palace of Fun (the twelfth point addressed below under the subtitle "Background"). There are others. Enjoy yourself.

1. Our hero is a man who held a highly confidential job of the most secret nature. He therefore has knowledge which is invaluable or highly dangerous depending which side of the fence he falls.
2. He resigns.
3. He is "computerised" to the "retired" file.
4. He is abducted from his home and transported unconscious to a place.
5. Is he abducted by "Us" or "Them"?
6. He awakens in a village.
7. He discovers that the village is a self-contained unit of our society with its own Council of Parliament.
8. He is treated with dangerous courtesy and invited to participate in all village activity.
9. He can stand for election on the Village Council and is invited to do so.
10. He is given a cottage with maid service and every conceivable modern amenity.

BUT: Every inch is bugged. His every move is watched constantly on closed-circuit television.

He has to have a Security Number to warrant an issue of village currency to enable him to buy food supplies, clothing, or even a glass of beer in the village pub.

In his cottage is a detailed map of the village with all exits clearly marked, but they are cut off by a deadly ray barrier.

Some of the residents encourage him to try and escape. Others attempt to dissuade him.

The favorite way to enter or exit The Village is by helicopter.

They are all known by numbers, and he cannot distinguish between a possible ally and a potential enemy.

Who are the Prisoners?

Who are the Captors?

All persons at all times behave with excessive normality against a background of sinister abnormality.

They all speak English. Sometimes a foreign language is heard in distant conversation but ceases upon his approach.

There are no outgoing telephone calls.

The Village Post Office returns all mail and cables—"Unknown."

11. Who then runs the village?
12. Is it "West" training him up to top indoctrination resistance?
13. "West" infiltrated by "East" trying to break him?
14. In any event—he is a prisoner.

The Action is on Three Levels

1. Our hero constantly probes to discover why he is a prisoner and who are his captors.
2. He strives by all means and at risk of death to escape.
3. He becomes involved with his captors and takes an active part in situations arising in their lives.

Background

1. The prison is a holiday-type village.

2. GEOGRAPHY

The village lies on a peninsula and covers five acres. It is completely isolated by a range of mountains that cut it off from the outside on the north-west and by dense forests on the north-east. For the rest it is surrounded by sea.

A flat beach a mile long is a prominent feature of the village.

There are cliffs and caves, and two old mines go deep in the bowels of the earth under the village.

The communal life of the village gravitates round thirteen main "blocks" of buildings, villas, bungalows, shops, etc.

3. COMMUNICATIONS

Telephone lines to the outside world are not available. There is no bus service, no railway station, taxis do not go outside the village. There is a closed-circuit T.V. service.

The Village was conceived from the beginning to be a cosmopolitan place, although English would always be the language of preference.

4. NAME

The village has no name. It is just the village or "here" or "this place."

5. TRANSPORT

The village has a taxi service of mini mokes with girl drivers. There are flying strip facilities (on the beach or lawns) for helicopters to take off or land.

6. SHOPPING

The village has a tiny number of shops. The most important is the General Store which supplies everything.

7. CURRENCY

The village uses its own. There are Units which are issued in lieu of any known currency. There is also a Credit Card system.

8. THE INMATES

There are two kinds—those who have been taken there and those who run it. But we cannot necessarily tell who is who.

9. INDUSTRY

There is no single industry in the village, but the people are kept busy doing all kinds of work. There is a factory manufacturing local requisites.

10. HOSPITAL

There is a hospital which is also in actual fact a conditioning centre using the latest methods. It is situated in the Castle which stands in a clearing by itself.

11. SURVEILLANCE

Constant. Television cameras record every move and activity both indoors and outside. Every type of modern electronic surveillance system is used to keep tabs on everyone.

12. AMUSEMENTS

All catered for. There are entertainment facilities of all kinds, from chess, dancing, gambling, film shows. There is a Palace of Fun to keep 'em happy. And amateur theatricals.

13. DEATH

The village has its own graveyard.

14. KEY BUILDINGS

These include:

a. The Labour Exchange, which assigns people varied tasks, "drafts" them to wherever they are wanted, organizes and runs the inmates.

b. The Citizen's Advice Bureau. Here all the inmates' problems can be solved.

c. The Town Hall. The municipal office and headquarters of the chairman.

d. The Palace of Fun.

e. The Hospital.

15. NEWSPAPER

The village produces its own.

16. T.V.—RADIO

The village has its own units, being particularly concerned with local news.

WHISTLING IN THE WIND

The Prisoner is Patrick McGoohan's baby, and it has been documented that even the theme music, credited to Ron Grainer, was created by McGoohan. According to the film librarian, Tony Sloman, McGoohan walked into Wilfred Thompson's cutting room one day and whistled what is now the main theme music of the series. McGoohan didn't write music, so Ron Grainer was hired to transcribe McGoohan's ideas. Of course Grainer deserves much credit for orchestrating the music and getting it in good shape. But the original idea, according to Sloman, was McGoohan's. Did this man ever sleep?

MEET THE PRESS

When *The Prisoner* was about to air in Great Britain, the press was invited to a special screening of "Arrival." McGoohan, dressed in his kosho uniform and wearing a Russian hat, was determined to turn the tables on the press. After the screening he brought the journalists to a room that included items such as a penny-farthing bicycle and the entire prison cage from "Once Upon a Time." McGoohan didn't answer any questions but instead asked questions of the press—asked them what they thought about Rover, the penny-farthing, and other aspects of the show. He asked many of these questions while standing in the prison, looking out through the bars. The press ended up getting very little information, which—considering the fact that they were not allowed at Portmeirion or on the studio set—made their reporting job impossible.

BUY BONDS

Three actors who played Number Two also appeared in James Bond movies. Guy Doleman ("Arrival") appeared in *Thunderball*. George Baker ("Arrival") was in *On Her Majesty's Secret Service*. And Colin Gordon ("A. B. and C." and "The General") performed in *Casino Royale*.

WHO'S IDEA WAS THIS, ANYWAY?

Most people are led to understand that Patrick McGoohan was the sole creative force behind *The Prisoner*, although it appears possible that George Markstein (the script editor) came up with the original idea. Markstein worked with McGoohan on *Secret Agent* and supposedly

By the time "Fall Out" was conceived, script editor George Markstein had left the show.

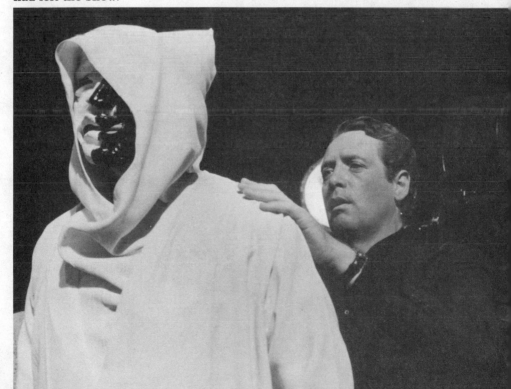

revealed the idea to McGoohan during a filming of the spy series. McGoohan then sold the idea as his own to Lew Grade, chief executive at ITC.

Whether or not Markstein gave birth to the idea of *The Prisoner*, the series took on the force of Patrick McGoohan's personality—so much so that McGoohan and Markstein had a falling-out over the final shape of the series (and the details of how Number One would be revealed in the final episode). McGoohan's case won out, and Markstein left the show. The last four episodes—"Do Not Forsake Me Oh My Darling," "Living in Harmony," "The Girl Who Was Death," and "Fall Out"—do not credit Markstein as script editor. (Of course, while they were the last four episodes to be completed, they were not the last four to be aired.)

This should not belittle Markstein's contribution to *The Prisoner*. He was in many ways as responsible as McGoohan for making *The Prisoner* come to life. For most of the series McGoohan and Markstein were collaborators in the truest sense of the word. But they were a strange pair. Scriptwriter Vincent Tilsley, in an interview conducted with Mark Goodacre, wondered how the "sensitive" Markstein and the "egocentric" McGoohan "got together in the first place." Knowing them both, he said "it was inevitable they would argue."

And they continued to argue, years after the series had been put to bed. Markstein said it was his idea; McGoohan said it was his. Markstein said that Number Six was John Drake; McGoohan denied it. And in a statement of what may be frustration, Markstein is on the record as saying *The Prisoner* was "the biggest load of rubbish."

DON'T ASK

Patrick McGoohan, when making *The Prisoner*, never revealed the identity of Number One to any member of the cast or crew.

YOU DON'T SAY. . . .

Members of the cast and crew were not allowed to say the word "television" on the set (or at least in front of Patrick McGoohan). McGoohan reportedly believed that people working on television shows were more willing to compromise their standards than people working on theatrical films.

MONEY MATTERS

Each episode of *The Prisoner* was budgeted at £75,000 ($187,500 in U.S. dollars), which was the most ever granted a television show at the time. Patrick McGoohan reportedly received £2,000 per week ($5,000 in U.S. dollars), as well as a share in the profits. This made him the highest-paid actor on television.

PRACTICAL ORDER

When *The Prisoner* first aired on British TV, the episodes were scheduled according to a rule of practicality: if it's finished, we'll air it. While ITC released the series in a theoretical final order to overseas TV stations, they didn't have that luxury in Great Britain, seeing as how several of the episodes were still being produced on the date they were intended to air. The order of the first screening, then—which tells more about the production process than any kind of sequential integrity—is given below. The sequence in which they aired in the United States is given in parenthesis.

 1. "Arrival" (1)
 2. "The Chimes of Big Ben" (2)
 3. "A. B. and C." (3)
 4. "Free for All" (4)
 5. "Schizoid Man" (5)
 6. "The General" (6)
 7. "Many Happy Returns" (7)
 8. "Dance of the Dead" (8)
 9. "Checkmate" (11)
10. "Hammer into Anvil" (14)
11. "It's Your Funeral" (10)
12. "A Change of Mind" (13)
13. "Do Not Forsake Me Oh My Darling" (9)
14. "Living in Harmony" (12)
15. "The Girl Who Was Death" (15)
16. "Once Upon a Time" (16)
17. "Fall Out" (17)

CHAPTER THREE

THE GREAT DEBATES

The true fan of *The Prisoner* is in many ways the privileged member of a debating society. It's impossible to address all the various debates in this chapter, although we've tried to tackle the most controversial and the most potent. It is not our intent to solve any of these debates, simply to set the boundaries of the discussion. While our bias will inevitably show through, we recognize that *The Prisoner* has survived intact over the past twenty years because the debates survive. Join us.

WHO IS NUMBER SIX?

Patrick McGoohan quit his role as John Drake in *Secret Agent* (*Danger Man* in the U.K.) to take on the role of Number Six in *The Prisoner*. Considering this, many people see a connection between the two characters—some go so far as to assert that John Drake is Number Six. There are many bits of evidence to support their claim.

McGoohan, however, has always maintained that John Drake and Number Six have nothing in common. In a somewhat perplexing statement, he said about Number Six: "He was never called John Drake, he just happened to look like him." McGoohan has also claimed that, if possible, he would have preferred Number Six be played by someone other than Patrick McGoohan, to avoid the inevitable connections be-

Was Number Six meant to be John Drake of *Secret Agent*? Or did the two characters simply look alike?

tween the two characters. Why has McGoohan remained so emphatic in his claim that Number Six was not John Drake?

The answer may have monetary overtones. If Number Six was indeed John Drake, the creators of *Secret Agent* would have a financial interest in the use of John Drake's character in *The Prisoner*. They would certainly expect some sort of royalty. Besides that, it may be that McGoohan believed that any connection with *Secret Agent* only served to weaken the impact of *The Prisoner*. The debate is a little mundane, and McGoohan may have felt that it would interfere with the complex philosophical problems that are addressed allegorically. McGoohan never expected viewers to understand *The Prisoner*, but he did hope that some of his message would get through. That, more than the monetary reasons, is most likely why McGoohan has so adamantly refused to encourage the debate and to state bluntly that Number Six was not John Drake. (It is also argued convincingly that McGoohan wanted to escape typecasting as John Drake, secret agent.)

But the debate will continue to rage, for various reasons. If McGoohan was so adamantly against the comparisons with *Secret Agent*, why would he allow the casting of an actor named John Drake in the episode "The Girl Who Was Death"? Why, too, would he have a character in that same episode assume the name of Potter (John Drake's confidant in *Secret Agent*) and give that role to the same actor who played Potter in *Secret Agent*? Obviously some of the comparisons are encouraged within the show itself. And to top it off, several people involved with the creation of *The Prisoner* are quick to make comparisons with *Secret Agent*. George Markstein has stated for the record that Number Six was John Drake, no doubt about it. And Jack Shampan, who was the art director for the series, remembers his first meeting with Patrick McGoohan and producer David Tomblin. He was asked to "chat with [Tomblin and McGoohan] about doing a continuation of *Danger Man* that they were toying with the idea of calling *The Prisoner*."

For our money, it's six of one, half a dozen of the other.

THE "LIVING IN HARMONY" DEBATE

In 1968 the United States was in the heat of the Vietnam War. Timothy Leary was busy telling people to "turn on, tune in, and drop out." Draft cards were burned as readily as bras, and the entire nation was positioned for change. Nixon started his enemy list.

This is the milieu in which *The Prisoner* came to television. Many people have quite rightly seen *The Prisoner* as an essay on its time period, a television show that thoughtfully explored the ideas of revolt. There was one episode of *The Prisoner*, however, that was linked more directly to the time period than the others. It is the allegorical western "Living in Harmony," and on the initial release of the series in 1968 it was left unaired, internally censored by the television network, CBS, itself.

In justifying its decision not to broadcast, CBS held that the portrayal of characters under the influence of hallucinogenic drugs was in violation of broadcast ethics. That may have been a factor in the censorship decision, but many people who have now seen the episode are starting to ask a few questions. First of all, the hallucinogens in this episode are portrayed in a negative light: they are used against Number Six in one more attempt to break his spirit. Second, although the entire episode is a hallucination, it is not known to the viewer as such until the end of the program. There is nothing in this episode that condones the use of such drugs or makes the consumption of hallucinogens appear attractive; just the opposite. Finally, there are many other episodes in the series that are much more aggressive in their portrayal of mind-altering drugs. In "A. B. and C.," "The Schizoid Man," "A Change of Mind," and "Once Upon a Time," drugs are much more of a factor in the story line; yet these episodes were aired without a hitch. What gives?

"Living in Harmony" is perhaps the most subversive episode in the series, and it deals allegorically with an issue that had much relevance to a country torn by the ethics of a military draft: What responsibility does an individual have to enforce the laws of his country? In this episode Number Six refuses to wear a badge or carry a gun for the good of the town of Harmony. He is subjected to incredible pressures to serve his community, and although he does eventually wear a badge and carry a gun, he does it for reasons that have nothing to do with those of the community. This cut a little close to home, containing obvious parallels to the Vietnam draft experience. Most close observers of *The Prisoner* now consider the Vietnam parallel, not the drug issue, to be the primary reason "Living in Harmony" was not shown to the U.S. public during 1968. Indeed, official spokesmen for both CBS and ITC are on the record as saying that the Vietnam issue killed the episode.

There may be one more reason CBS paid especially close attention to this particular episode. Most of *The Prisoner* episodes are set in The Village or in London—distant locations to U.S. audiences and often fantastic and unreal. "Living in Harmony" is set in the mythical American West, a location that is not only within the U.S. borders, but one that has been used repeatedly for moral tales of good and evil, right and wrong. Although there are subversive elements within all episodes of *The Prisoner*, they are more easily identified and understood when played out in a western boot town called Harmony.

"Living in Harmony" was the only episode not to play during the initial run in the United States. Note that Number Six is not wearing a gun.

DID NUMBER SIX ACTUALLY RESIGN?

A curious debate, posed fairly recently, asks what seems at first to be an irrelevant question: Is Number Six still employed and working as a spy during his stay in The Village? Most viewers would agree that Number Six resigned and, because of that, was incarcerated in The Village. But there is some intriguing evidence that Number Six is indeed a plant, sent to The Village by his superiors for espionage purposes. If this is true,

Number Two in "Hammer Into Anvil" believes that Number Six was planted in The Village by the authorities to test security measures. Was he right?

then the paranoid atmosphere of The Village takes on a dimension of incredible proportions. Not only do we wonder who in The Village is trustworthy; we now must decide whether we can trust Number Six himself.

The place to begin this debate is in the episode "Hammer into Anvil," in which Number Two is convinced that Number Six is a plant, assigned to The Village by The Village's authorities to spy on Number Two. The initial screening of this episode makes it appear that Number Six is playing a devious game, that he has turned the tables on Number Two in order to take revenge on Number Two's sadistic handling of a fellow Villager. But what if this is no game? What if Number Six is indeed carrying out his orders? What, indeed?

We have plenty of evidence that Number Six was an accomplished spy. Besides the obvious espionage techniques employed in "Hammer into Anvil," he is seen cracking complicated codes in such episodes as "Do Not Forsake Me Oh My Darling" (the proper projection of photographic slides to reveal a location). In that same episode he is known to others by secret code names, be it another number (ZM73) or a fictitious name (Schmidt, Duvall). But the question remains: Is he still a spy, or has he resigned?

The most compelling evidence that he did not resign is held in the answer to the question, Who is Number One? The answer to this question, almost unanimously, is that Number Six is Number One. But there's a lot of debate over what that means. Could it be possible that Number Six is Number One in the most obvious sense: that he controls The Village and is the ultimate authority?

If we allow ourselves to carry this thought so far, there must be a motive. Why would Number Six subject himself to the various tortures within The Village? The answer must have something to do with national security: Number Six has been placed in The Village to test its security. In "Do Not Forsake Me Oh My Darling," we understand that the breaking of security is of prime importance to The Villagers. (Number Two in that episode is delighted to discover that he may have stumbled across a method—mind transference—that would break the security of any nation.)

This theory is appealing and puts several pieces of the puzzle in place. We never know what information is in Number Six's head, and neither does any Number Two. But Number Two is always under orders to treat Number Six with a special respect and not to destroy him or his mind. These orders, which are given by the ultimate authorities, protect Number Six within The Village. Why would Number One be so careful to protect Number Six unless Number Six was actually working for Number One (or is Number One himself)?

The final bit of evidence to support this theory is contained in the last scene of the last episode. Number Six, now in London and apparently free from The Village, leaves The Butler at his house in London. The door opens automatically, much like the doors in The Village. But Number Six pays that no mind. Indeed, it's as if he expects it. Most have thought this confirmed the fact that there is no escape from The Village. But what if it means that Number Six has been a Villager all along? (To be fair, there is some question whether or not Number Six is even aware that the door opened automatically.)

There's much here of interest. And while it's somewhat worthwhile to entertain the idea, it's something else entirely to believe it. The connotations are simply too great. It's as if a big trick has been played on the viewer, and it leads to one incredibly downbeat conclusion: nobody can be trusted, not even the man we have come to respect for his integrity, his individuality, and his persistence against the evils of society. This is a paranoid worldview, offering no exit.

It is difficult, however, to discount this theory; many of Number Six's rebellious actions can be considered tests of national security. However, there are a few instances in which Number Six undermines certain aspects of Village Society that—if he were actually a high authority in The Village—would be in his interest to protect.

The most obvious example of such an act is in "The General," when Number Six goes to great lengths to subvert a speed-learning tactic that could only have been authorized by top authorities. In that same episode he intentionally destroys a Village computer (and he destroys another one in "Dance of the Dead"). In "It's Your Funeral" Number Six succeeds in combating a plot to kill off an over-the-hill Number Two—a plot that, again, could only have been authorized by top officials. While these examples could be twisted even further to support the Number Six-as-working-spy theory, they would be twisted to extremely paranoid dimensions.

In the end the debate works like a logic puzzle, forcing the attentive viewer to review the various situations and see how they fit the theory. It's certainly valid as one interpretation of *The Prisoner*. However, as Patrick McGoohan has said, there are thousands of such interpretations, and that's the way he intended it.

IS *THE PRISONER* SUBVERSIVE?

One of the more interesting debates to be launched in recent years concerns the potentially subversive nature of *The Prisoner*. The most radical proponents of this debate insist that *The Prisoner* is a call for political action, for revolution. Those who engage in the debate are usually in one of two camps. Some believe that *The Prisoner* is a descriptive series, allegorically identifying key problems within society, and

Did Patrick McGoohan intend *The Prisoner* to be a subversive attack on modern society?

is concerned primarily with big ethical, religious, and artistic issues. Others believe it is both a descriptive and a prescriptive series, identifying the problems and then going one step further: providing an agenda— or at least an example—for political action.

Everyone agrees with the allegorical intent of the series. *The Prisoner* should not be categorized as a work of science fiction. It is not a fantasy series, in the sense that we are encouraged to escape from the mundane realities of present life. *The Prisoner* is an allegorical statement about modern-day political realities. It is about the world we live in. The debate concerns whether the intent of *The Prisoner* was to 1) creatively explore the nature of modern man, or 2) change the world. There are good arguments on both sides.

Those who believe *The Prisoner* is basically descriptive have a good deal of respect for the main issue within the series: the struggle between the individual and society. These people see Number Six as the extreme representation of the individual and The Village as the extreme representation of society. Considering that they are so extreme, the basic conflict rings clear as a bell: to exist, society must maintain a certain degree of control over the individual (as Number Two says to Number Six in "Once Upon a Time": "Society is a place where people live together; the lone wolf belongs in the wilderness"). The individual, on the other hand, struggles to maintain his or her freedom, always battling the collective desire of the society to restrict those freedoms ("I am not a number; I am a person"). Many people believe this to be an age-old conflict and basically irreconcilable. To them, *The Prisoner* is one of the best creative expressions of this conflict.

Those who insist that *The Prisoner* is a subversive political statement are much more attuned to the modern-day problems addressed by the series. To them, the key issues are those raised by a society that has become increasingly sophisticated technologically and is willing to use those technological advances to assert an unfair authority over the individual. It is Number Six who says, "The problem with science is that it can be perverted," and much of the series—to the subversive element—not only demonstrates the perversions of science, but goes one step beyond, showing ways for the individual to rebel and engage in acts of revolt. To them, Number Six is a type of modern-day prophet, leading the willing to a new promised land.

The debate is fascinating, especially considering that most casual viewers considered *The Prisoner* to be nothing more than a strange kind of entertainment. But is the debate important? In many ways it is of vital importance, if for nothing else than a television series advocating political revolt played on network television during the late 1960s. The question remains, however: Was the series intended to be subversive?

Certainly the series attacks many of the institutions that are held in some esteem: democratic elections, citizen groups, educational systems, the courts, and so forth. But while the series may be quick to attack these institutions, it never offers any real alternatives. (Even anarchy is ridiculed in the final episode of *The Prisoner*.) And although that doesn't make the criticisms less valid, it does add support to those who believe this to be a descriptive allegory, one that creatively identifies irreconcilable and timeless conflicts in society.

But what's to be made over this guy who revolted, resisted, fought, held fast, maintained, destroyed resistance, and overcame coercion? Is he some kind of role model? Is he some kind of prophet?

It is hard to escape the fact that, yes, he is a role model and perhaps a prophet, and that *The Prisoner* advocates (if only by example) rebellion—even if that rebellion is waged against hopeless odds. The rebellion of *The Prisoner* is not unlike the rebellion of Thoreau as articulated in his works on civil disobedience or the rebellion of Martin Luther King as described in *Letters from Birmingham Jail*. It is a call to action in that it demands that the viewer question his or her situation, and it encourages the viewer not only to question authority, but to undermine authority—especially when that authority has gone too far.

It is important to note that *The Prisoner* does not envision any type of utopia, nor does it advocate any kind of organized rebellion. It is solidly grounded in a perpetual struggle between the right of the individual to be individual and the right of the state to govern. The struggle between the individual and society is seen as a perpetual struggle, but one that must be taken seriously and fought. If the individual fights, he or she is guaranteed only that the war will continue; there is no guarantee or hope that the war can be won. If the individual doesn't fight, however, the war is over; the individual loses, and the future looks very bleak indeed.

DOES NUMBER SIX ESCAPE?

Of all the debates in this chapter, this is undoubtedly the most controversial and compelling. McGoohan has added his own fuel to the fire, saying Number Six doesn't escape, that "freedom is a myth." And while most of the debaters side with McGoohan, there are other interpretations that are still valid and worth discussing.

From physical evidence, you can believe what you want. Number Six does get out of The Village and does end up back in London. That's clear. However, the ending sequence of the last episode is identical with the opening sequence of the first, leaving some with the impression that the entire process will repeat itself—that Number Six will actually end up in The Village once again. Others see it as simply driving home the point of the allegory. Number Six may escape The Village, but London represents just as severe a prison. They point to the fact that Number Six, after arriving in London, is still identified as "The Prisoner." These are compelling reasons to believe that Number Six is doomed to an eternal struggle for his freedom, but there are other equally compelling reasons to believe he has earned and been granted his freedom.

Those who believe that Number Six escaped consider him a heroic figure, a type of superman. From the opening sequence of the first episode, we understand that Number Six has one objective: to resign his position at the secret service and thus gain peace of mind. He is not allowed to resign so easily, and thus he is put through seventeen episodes of tests. Like a martial artist faced with seventeen rooms of death, he survives each test and earns his freedom. Although London may be every bit as much a prison as The Village, one individual has earned his right, through pure revolt, to be an individual. That individual is then left with a choice: "To lead us, or go." Number Six both leads and goes.

Number Six leads three people out of The Village: a hippielike revolutionary, a middle-aged bureaucrat who "bites the hand that feeds him," and a silent butler who recognizes true authority and follows that authority's lead. Number Six leads them to London and then lets them go to fend for themselves. And Number Six, having led his followers out of The Village, drives off a free man. Or so it seems.

Rover makes it very difficult for Number Six to successfully execute any escape.

The debate will go on forever. The shooting script to "Fall Out" only adds to the confusion, for it differs radically with a few important details at the end. In the end of the show that was produced, Number Six leaves The Butler at the door and takes off again in his Lotus 7. The words "The Prisoner" appear underneath him, and thus we are led to believe that the cycle may repeat itself; that he doesn't escape. In the script, however, Number Six walks into his London apartment with The Butler and closes the door. The words "The Prisoner" do not appear on the screen. Instead, the music swells at the end with the words "O Hear the Word of the Lord," which is more in keeping with the prophecy aspect; and it further encourages one to believe that some type of freedom has been secured.

WHO RUNS THE VILLAGE?

In the original documents that were composed by George Markstein to introduce *The Prisoner* to potential screenwriters, it is clear that we should never know for certain who runs The Village. It is either "Us" or "Them." If Number Six is an agent for the British government, the "Us" is most

Is Number Two working for "Us" or "Them"?

likely the Brits or, more generally, the "West." The "Them" is most likely
the enemy: the Soviets or, more generally, the "East."

During the past twenty years of serious talk about *The Prisoner*, three
more theories have been added to the "Us" or "Them" theories. Possibly
"Us" and "Them" have come together, and The Village is run by some
kind of futuristic world government. Or perhaps it's not a government
at all, but a multinational corporation. Finally, a peripheral branch of
Prisoner scholars have speculated that The Village may be run by extra-
terrestrials. What gives?

Number Six is interested in the debate: he wants to know who his
captors are. The big episode for speculation on this issue is "The Chimes
of Big Ben," in which Number Two claims that it doesn't really matter
and speculates that the world is heading toward some kind of unified
politic. If we knew who ran The Village, we might get answers to some
other questions, such as "Why is it so important that Number Six be held
together, body and soul? Why don't they just extract what information
they want and be rid of him?"

The theory of some kind of unified world power is held together
through some circumstantial evidence. Obviously many different coun-
tries are represented in The Village; many different languages are spoken.
As the taxi driver says to Number Six in "Arrival": "It's very cosmopolitan."
But if it is a world power, it's not at all clear why the information in
Number Six's head would be so priceless. The most damning evidence
toward a world-power theory is given in "Do Not Forsake Me Oh My
Darling," in which Number Two fantasizes about the ability to "break
the security of any nation" and talks about spy swaps. A world power
would not be that concerned with breaking the security of individual
nations; and it would have nobody with which to swap spies.

The "Us" aspect of the debate is also hard to justify—there's simply
too much working against it. In "Arrival" we learn that Cobb—an old
associate of Number Six—is working for "new masters." It would be
difficult to argue that the new masters were British or of the West.
Apparently he is working for "Them," and it is "They" who run The
Village (it is also interesting that Cobb's cohort in this episode is a Slavic
woman named Nadia). Also, if it is "Us" who runs The Village, it would
be easy enough to do away with Number Six. In fact, the information
within Number Six's head would make him a security risk, and it may
be best simply to terminate him. However, there is some support left to
the "Us" theory. We have some reason to believe that many British
espionage agents are now working for The Village. Certainly Fotheringay
and The Colonel in "The Chimes of Big Ben" are working for The Village.
And it is possible (but by no means clear) that the British superiors
introduced in "Many Happy Returns" and in "Do Not Forsake Me Oh My
Darling" are in on Number Six's incarceration. The evidence, however,

seems to be something like seventy-thirty against the possibility that it is "Us" who run the village.

Then it must be "Them." Not so fast. If it is "Them," it would appear that no punches would be pulled in Number Six's interrogation. They want information, and they would probably take any means to extract that information. The only reason for keeping Number Six alive and kicking would be to have him turn double agent on "Us"—something that would be hard to put over, seeing as how Number Six resigned from the service. On the other hand, there are more consistencies to the "Them" theory than there are to the "Us" theory. In "Many Happy Returns" Number Six is returned to The Village by a pilot who evidently does not work for the British. In "Free for All" the female Number Two asks that The Village official who is taking off in a helicopter give her regards to "the homeland." There are plenty of other instances where "They" seem to be in control, but the problem still remains as to why "They" feel it so important to keep Number Six intact.

Perhaps "They" is not a government at all, but a multinational corporation. This theory has been getting lots of attention these days, and it appears to have some validity. A multinational corporation would have an interest in keeping Number Six alive. They want the basic information, sure, but they would also have need of the expertise of a man who knew the inner workings of Western security measures. They would be more interested in having Number Six lead them (as they ask him to do in "Fall Out") than would a state government. The multinational corporation theory also helps to explain the great efficiency and expense that went into the creation of The Village. A state government probably couldn't get its act together to fund The Village concept or run it so efficiently. It also helps to explain all the different languages that are spoken—by both prisoners and wardens.

Although the multinational corporation theory helps explain some curious aspects of The Village, it is never really broached outright in the series. Seventeen episodes were broadcast, covering topics from speed learning to democracy to medical abuses to judicial procedures. Not one episode took on the idea of multinational corporations (although it could certainly provide inspiration for some future episode of *The Prisoner*). In order to argue this theory, you've got to dig a little too deeply.

There's more tangible evidence to support the extraterrestrial theory, although this is admittedly on the fringe of *Prisoner* thought. The extraterrestrial theory was developed to help explain the rocket ship that is launched during "Fall Out." It can be argued that Number Six was taken not to some part of the world, but to another planet. To further support this theory, people have noted the various uses of clones in several episodes—most strikingly the clone of Number Six himself in both "Schizoid Man" and "Fall Out." Although we have to admit that the rocket ship and the clones are puzzling, this is a difficult theory to take seriously.

In the end, we cannot know who runs The Village—and we are not supposed to. The episodes often tease us with hints here or there, but this was intended to be an enigma. The people who run The Village are the authorities, be they governmental, multinational, or alien. They are the people who carry the big stick, and they are not afraid to use it.

THE PROPER ORDER

It would be possible to fill this entire book with arguments on the proper ordering of the episodes in *The Prisoner*, but it would serve little purpose. It's worthwhile noting that a frustrating debate rages on this topic. We can set the boundaries of the debate here. As far as the actual ordering goes, we'll leave that to you.

We only know three things for sure. "Arrival" is the first episode. "Once Upon a Time" is the sixteenth episode, and "Fall Out" is the final episode. Flashbacks from "Arrival" and "Free for All" are shown in the episode "Do Not Forsake Me Oh My Darling," which means that it has to be placed after those episodes. Other than that, the order is up for grabs.

There are two "official" orders: the order in which the episodes were first screened in the U.K. and the order in which they were first screened overseas (we'll call it the U.S. order). Of the two "official" orders, the U.S. order is probably the most official, seeing as how some episodes were delayed during their U.K. broadcast because they were not completed. The U.S. order is the one used in the episode guide.

But just because an order is "official" doesn't make it right, and many people have spent much time trying to reorder the episodes. There are plenty of ways to do this.

One of the most popular is to order the episodes by dates and time periods that are evident within the series itself. For example, in "Do Not Forsake Me Oh My Darling" we know that Number Six has been away for a year. In "Many Happy Returns" we know that he arrives in London on March 18, and that he had been sailing for twenty-five days. In "Schizoid Man" we know that Number Six's various ordeals started on February 10. Through a close examination of time periods, people have been able to create a fairly logical, sequential order.

Another tactic is to examine the way in which Number Six is treated by the authorities. The reasoning goes that the interrogation of Number Six gets riskier and more intense as the series progresses. In such thinking, an episode like "A. B. and C."—which is officially shown as the third episode—is placed much later in the series, because Number Two appears quite willing to risk the life of Number Six.

Denise Huckley plays The Maid in "Dance of the Dead," the eighth episode of the series. Many believe that this episode should come earlier.

Another popular method is to order the episodes by paying close attention to conversations. In an episode like "Dance of the Dead," officially shown as the eighth episode, Number Six says, "I'm new here." Perhaps, then, it should be aired earlier. There are numerous other such instances.

The truth is the producers were probably not all that concerned with order. This was a television series of seventeen episodes. It had a final ending that was unique, but other than that it was most likely treated as a series of interchangeable exploits within The Village. It is worthwhile to think about the order and to create your own. But this is a debate that will never be resolved.

CHAPTER FOUR

WHAT DOES IT ALL MEAN?

I wanted to have controversy, arguments, fights, discussions, people in anger, waving fists in my face.

—Patrick McGoohan, discussing the meaning of "Fall Out"

Questions are a burden for others. Answers are a prison for oneself.

—Village sign

Anybody who has been fortunate enough to view even one episode of *The Prisoner* is going to ask the question, What in the world is going on here? It's not an easy question to answer; indeed, millions of viewers have sat transfixed before the TV screen without the slightest idea as to what this show is all about. That, of course, is intentional (as McGoohan himself makes clear in the quote that leads off this chapter) and is part of the series's charm and legacy.

The real question is not what the show is all about, but whether it is worth the effort to find a meaning in a television series that is intentionally controversial, argumentative, and obscure. Is it worth getting angry and waving fists in McGoohan's face? We think it is.

The fascination of *The Prisoner* has been kept aflame for the past few decades not because it was some nostalgic landmark that warmed the heart, but because it was like no other television series ever made. It stands alone as television's greatest intellectual achievement and, we believe, its proudest moment.

But what does it mean? McGoohan has described the meaning in two words: "an allegory." From that it has been argued that *The Prisoner* is about nuclear holocaust, that it is about religious prophecy, that it is about man's inhumanity to man, or that it simply is. Like great art, it is

163

able to sustain multiple interpretations—each one valid and each with advocates. We refuse to force any one meaning on *The Prisoner,* for that in many ways defeats the basic premise of the show. There are no perfect answers, there are only perfect questions.

THE NATURE OF MAN

"And now I take it that you are prepared to meet Number One, Sir?"

—The President, "Fall Out"

Those who insist on finding meaning in *The Prisoner* must begin their inquiry with the most persistent enigma of the series: the identity of Number One. For sixteen episodes the viewer had been teased into expecting some type of major revelation, some answer to a question that

Many interpret *The Prisoner* as a battle between the good and the evil side of man.

had been posed week in and week out. The answer was finally provided in "Fall Out," but it was an answer few were expecting and even fewer could comprehend. It had little to do with ultimate answers and much to do with the nature of man.

Number One is revealed at the end of the show to be ... Number Six himself. The close observer knew this all along. In every episode Number Six would ask, "Who is Number One?" and in every episode he received the answer, "You are Number Six" (or, more emphatically, You are, Number Six"). In every episode we could tell that Number Six had a London home with the address of 1 Buckingham Place. But even with all these clues, it was somewhat shocking to learn in "Fall Out" that Number Six was indeed Number One. It was an answer, but what did it mean?

Patrick McGoohan has stated for the record that Number One is the evil side of ourselves. Most *Prisoner* devotees subscribe to this theory, and it does appear to answer most of the allegorical problems addressed in the series. The good side of man is held prisoner by the evil side of man. Both coexist in the same body and in the same body politic. It is this that makes us human and causes anxiety. Society may be charged with upholding the good against the evil, but society is in the end an institution comprised of human beings. There is no escape from our basic human dilemma. This, to many, is the ultimate message and meaning of *The Prisoner*.

Although this is a reasonable interpretation of the series, encouraged by McGoohan himself, there is something more primary at work here than good and evil. There is another battle raging in *The Prisoner*, another study of man's nature that is more biological and, ultimately, more challenging.

When Number Six starts tearing at the mask of Number One, he is first confronted with the mask of a chimpanzee and, after that has been ripped off, with the image of himself. Perhaps the true conflict of *The Prisoner* and the more accurate insight into the nature of man is embodied in these two images: ape and man. Good and evil, in this theory, is but a caricature of the real conflict, which is between the animal instincts and that which is not animal (intelligence, creativity).

If we're looking for some kind of message here, it would appear that *The Prisoner* is asking us to confront this dual nature of mankind head on and to reconcile it. There's a warning in "Once Upon a Time" that is evolutionary in its structure. Number Two, as if in a lecture, scrawls the most important points of Degree Absolute on a blackboard:

1. Find missing link.
2. Put it together.
3. (if fail) Bang.

These points can only be understood in terms of the animal conflict. And the warning seems to say that, if we don't put it all together—if we don't integrate these two opposing aspects of man's nature—we're bound to self-destruct.

INDIVIDUAL AGAINST SOCIETY

"You are a member of The Village.
You are a unit of society."

—Number Two to Number Six, "Once Upon a Time"

The most obvious meaning concerns the battle of an individual against the oppression of society. There is little argument here. Number Six represents a man who refuses to conform. The Village represents a society that demands conformity. This is a timeless theme, and many people interpret *The Prisoner* as but one more attempt to confront the theme.

Within this inevitable confrontation, there are several ways to interpret the message. The struggle between individual and society may simply be polarized, with Number Six representing the ultimate individual and The Village representing the ultimate society. There is no possible meeting of minds. For society to exist, it must negate the individual impulse; otherwise a type of unproductive anarchy will reign. For the individual to maintain his dignity and self, he must rebel against the dictates of society. In the most simplistic interpretation, then, *The Prisoner* dramatizes a timeless confrontation, unresolved. Nothing more, nothing less.

The message assumes additional dimensions if the viewer starts to take sides in the matter. Number Six is an attractive fellow, and most viewers will sympathize with his cause. Taken to the extreme, some people see *The Prisoner* as a call to individualism. Number Six, in the extreme, is a role model—someone to emulate. Others see Number Six as a kind of antihero: a troublemaker. While this is admittedly a minority point of view, a case can be made for the society against the whims of the individual, or The Village against Number Six. Such people argue that if Number Six had his way, the society would cease to exist. And what good would that do?

The most popular resolution to the conflict is to put Number Six on a higher pedestal, to see him as a type of superman or hero. In this respect Number Six is a man "magnificently equipped to lead us," as The President concedes in "Fall Out." But as also demonstrated in "Fall Out," the society refuses to hear the real message of Number Six, and thus the conflict continues. But is the society, as represented in *The Prisoner*, the perfect society? Or can society be changed?

The members of society are often portrayed as mindless automatons, willing to follow any lead.

A SIGN OF THE TIMES

*"Youth with its enthusiasms—which rebels against any
accepted norms—because it must, and we sympathize. It
may wear flowers in its hair and bells on its toes. . . ."*

—President to assembly, "Fall Out"

There's no escaping the fact that *The Prisoner* is a product of its times
—specifically, the late 1960s. And whether or not you subscribe to the
theory that *The Prisoner* is a study of its turbulent time period, it is
impossible to watch this series without thinking about days when revolution seemed possible and the status quo seemed doomed.

One of the explanations for *The Prisoner*'s popularity during the
late 1960s is that it captured the imagination of the counterculture. Number Six was an unyielding rebel, and rebellion was in the air. He refused
to buckle under to the authorities, he was determined to expose the
hypocrisies of the system, and he had to fight for every freedom, tooth
and nail. There were plenty of people, most of them young, who could
identify immediately with this character.

The makers of *The Prisoner* were undoubtedly aware of what was
going on in the world around them, and much of what was going on
was incorporated into the series. Technically the series looks like a 1960s
production: the rich, bright coloring of The Village and Villagers is consistent with the explosive coloring the 1960s, be it a Peter Max Volkswagen
or a Jimmy Hendrix poster. The crude special camera effects, especially
those intended to indicate an altered-mind state (see especially the party
scenes in "A. B. and C."), were not unlike those exploring hallucinogenic
experiences in Roger Corman's drive-in films. And in "Fall Out" the music
and the language (a Beatles' song and sixties slang) brings the relationship
between the series and the times up front, for those who missed it.

There is little question that *The Prisoner* supports many of the ideas
of the counterculture. "Living in Harmony" hit so close to home that it
wasn't aired in the United States. In "A Change of Mind" there is a strong
attack on the practice of lobotomy, and throughout the series there are
attacks on psychiatric medical treatments. This fits right into a time period
that was questioning the ideas of insanity and sanity, as popularized
through films like *King of Hearts* and books like *One Flew Over the Cuckoo's Nest*. And during a time when J. Edgar Hoover was keeping secret
files and Nixon was creating enemy lists, the paranoia—especially over
electronic means of surveillance—was great. And if there is one theme
that is hit hard throughout *The Prisoner*, it is the omnipresence of surveillance and the spirit of paranoia.

During the late 1960s, there was much speculation on mind-reading and telepathy.

But if *The Prisoner* is hip to the politics of the 1960s, it is decidedly unhip in terms of life-style. Drugs (excepting alcohol) are the enemy throughout. There is no argument for recreational drug use; just the opposite. Drugs are a weapon wielded without conscience by the authorities. Free love isn't addressed—even once—in the series, and there is some ambivalence toward women in general (in "Dance of the Dead" Number Six claims that he can't trust women; in other episodes he plays a chivalric role, defending damsels in distress). And numerous potshots are taken at the fashionable ideas of the sixties, be it encounter groups ("A Change of Mind"), abstract art openings ("The Chimes of Big Ben"), or the type of Zen Buddhism that is taught through motorcycle maintenance (Number Two in "Checkmate"; the kosho games).

THE END OF THE WORLD

"POP."

—Number Six to Number Two to Number Six, "Once Upon a Time"

Much has been made of *The Prisoner* as an apocalyptic statement—a warning about the end of the world. It may be. The best evidence for this theory, however, is contained in a bit of animation that, until recently, was considered "lost."

This is found at the end of the original credits, which can be seen on the videocassette "The Alternate Chimes of Big Ben." At the end of these credits, the world and the universe apparently explode as the word "POP" fills the screen. There is really very little that is subject to interpretation here; the universe does appear to explode.

But this "alternate" ending is just that—an alternate ending. It did not appear during any of the broadcast runs and does not now appear on any of the videocassettes (except, of course, on the alternate episode mentioned above). Is there anything within the series itself that would support an apocalyptic vision?

Sure there is, but you have to make some serious leaps of faith to tie it into a neat bow. The big evidence concerns the scientific dilemmas, which permeate the series. An important theme of *The Prisoner* is that science can be perverted. True scientists are usually treated with utmost sympathy and respect (one of the most noble characters in the series is the brilliant Dr. Seltzman in "Do Not Forsake Me Oh My Darling"). However, the people who apply the scientific principles are usually treated with contempt—be they psychiatrists, doctors, or people in power. In episode after episode we are exposed to power-hungry people in control of sophisticated technology.

The threat of atomic warfare is addressed directly only once in the series, by Dr. Seltzman, who speculates on whether the atom would have been split if the scientists understood the ramifications of that action. That's probably enough to orient *The Prisoner* in the nuclear debate, but not enough to interpret the series as a warning about nuclear destruction. In "The Girl Who Was Death" it can be assumed that the superrocket being launched by the mad scientist to destroy London is a nuclear weapon. Although played mostly for laughs, it does have an "end of London" theme. But for the threat of nuclear war to become the main message of *The Prisoner*, more evidence is necessary. And that evidence can only be found in "Fall Out."

When Number Six confronts Number One in "Fall Out," he finds the hooded figure in a highly guarded control room that may be construed as containing "the button." We know that at least one big rocket can be launched by the controls in that room—Number Six himself launches the rocket at the end of the episode. If we accept McGoohan's interpretation that Number One is "the evil side of man," it can be argued that in "Fall Out" the evil side of ourselves is at the controls of destruction. Number Six saves the day (and perhaps the world) by chasing the evil side out of the control room and taking over the controls. He then turns the destructive force into something positive—as a way to escape. If this was in a storybook that Number Six was reading to children, at the end of "Fall Out" he might very well say: "And that, children, is how I saved the world from the evil side of ourselves."

THE PROPHECY

"O Hear the Word of the Lord."

—Number Forty-eight, "Fall Out"

—Ezekiel 37:1–14

When Mary Morris, who played Number Two in "Dance of the Dead," was asked about the various meanings of *The Prisoner* in a 1985 interview, she replied that it might have some type of religious message and added that Patrick McGoohan was "a very religious man." There's a lot to speculate on here, and many observers have interpreted the religious symbolism and themes in a variety of interesting but often contradictory ways.

To get at what might be going on, it's best to concentrate on the Negro spiritual "Dry Bones." In many ways it plays as a theme song for the final episode, "Fall Out." "Dry Bones" ("The collarbone's connected to the neckbone/The neckbone's connected to the head bone/O hear the word of the Lord") is based on a biblical reference involving the prophet Ezekiel. In the Old Testament, Ezekiel comes into a valley of dry bones. The Lord asks Ezekiel to prophesy to the bones, to give them

There is much religious symbolism in *The Prisoner*. Did McGoohan see his character as a modern-day prophet?

life. After the prophecy, the bones do indeed come to life and form "an exceedingly large army."

The choice of the song "Dry Bones" was no accident. According to several production personnel, McGoohan was adamant about the use of this song, and many versions of it were researched before the final selection was made.

Those who are willing to entertain *The Prisoner* as some type of religious statement are able to find a simple message in one key word: "prophecy." *The Prisoner* suddenly becomes a prophetic exercise, a type of preaching to the masses. The prophet in this case would probably be McGoohan himself, and the "dry bones" would be the members of society who are living without hope and without thought. The prophecy becomes *The Prisoner* itself, designed to shake people up, to make them think, to breathe life into their bones. It also is a prophetic warning, full of fire and brimstone: Woe be to those who do not hear the word of *The Prisoner*.

The prophetic aspect of *The Prisoner* is not without power, and much of the other interpretations can fit neatly into its thesis: warnings of the end of the world; insights into contemporary political problems; debates between the individual and society. All of these could be components of the same prophecy, which is to get people moving, to get them mad, and, ultimately, to make them think

CHAPTER FIVE

TALKING WITH McGOOHAN

PATRICK McGOOHAN: BIOGRAPHICAL INFORMATION

Patrick McGoohan was born in the United States (in the Astoria district on Long Island), although his family returned to their farm in Ireland within a few months of his birth on March 19, 1928. McGoohan left school at sixteen and held a few odd jobs (in steel mills, at a bank, and at a chicken farm) before he took on the job of stage manager at the Sheffield Repertory Company. It was there that he became actively involved in the theater, and it was there that he met his future wife, Joan Drummond.

McGoohan performed bit and lead roles in over 200 plays at the Sheffield before he moved on to more prestigious theatrical roles at West End theaters during the mid-1950s. One of his first big breaks in the theater was landing the role of Starbuck in Orson Welles' *Moby Dick, Rehearsed* (Welles played the role of Ahab). McGoohan also ventured into some television work and, in 1955, started receiving bit roles in British film productions, including *Passage Home*, *I Am a Camera*, *The Dam Busters*, and *Zarak*.

In 1957, McGoohan was placed under contract with the Rank Organization to perform in motion pictures. He was often cast as a villain, and his roles became more and more important. While performing in

175

Rank productions such as *High Tide at Noon, Hell Driver*, and *Elephant Gun*, he also appeared in live television dramas for the BBC. In 1959, audiences and critics were paying attention to McGoohan: he was named Best TV Actor of the Year.

McGoohan, who was developing a reputation as an "angry young man," was approached by Lew Grade of the Independent Television Corporation (ITC) to play the lead role in a new television series, *Danger Man* (*Secret Agent* in the U.S.). McGoohan accepted the role of John Drake, and it became a popular British (but not international) television show. The first round of *Secret Agent* episodes terminated in 1961. Then, the James Bond movies hit on an international scale (McGoohan was offered the role of James Bond but turned it down) and *Danger Man* resumed production in 1964. This time, the program became an international hit, and McGoohan became an international star.

In 1966, McGoohan began to tire of the John Drake character, and proposed the idea of *The Prisoner* to Lew Grade at ITC. In the twenty years since *The Prisoner*, McGoohan has been in films such as *Scanners* and *Baby*; he has been making guest appearances on television shows such as *Murder, She Wrote*; and he has been performing on stage (most recently on Broadway in *Pack of Lies*). McGoohan now makes his home in Southern California.

(The following interview was originally printed in the summer/fall 1985 issue of New Video *magazine. The interviewer was Barrington Calia, and it is reprinted with permission of* New Video *Magazine.)*

Enjoying the lead in the Broadway play *Pack of Lies*, McGoohan agreed to an interview with us after we contacted him through the play's producer, Arthur Cantor. Preceded by a reputation of being "abrasive" (an adjective he's heard others use to describe him), easily agitated, and uncompromising, McGoohan and I engaged in the following discourse as I proceeded with an assumed air of masochism: about to interview a man that doesn't like to give interviews. Indeed, life imitates art during this ironic interaction, often amusingly analogous to the dialogue presented in McGoohan's humanistic allegory.

He invited me in. I shook his hand, was offered a seat, then eagerly began; wasting none of the time he was gracious enough to allot me. At the behest of *New Video* magazine, *The Prisoner* was about to complete his sentence; on the printed page.

Barrington Calia: What is the symbolic significance of the bicycle insignia used in *The Prisoner*?

Patrick McGoohan: Progress! It's an ironic symbol of progress. The penny-farthing bicycle represents a simpler age. We live in an era where science is advancing so quickly, you don't even have time to learn about the latest innovations before something new arises; making what you've learned obsolete. It's the same with the newspapers. They're so busy cranking out information that before you get a chance to digest it, they're cramming something else down your throat! Everything is moving very fast, possibly too fast . . . before its time.

BC: Is *The Prisoner* John Drake, secret agent (the main character from the espionage/action television series from the 1960s)?

McG: (emphatically) No! I was asked to create an action series because of the popularity of *Danger Man* and *Secret Agent*; both of which I starred in. Lew Grade called me into his office and asked me to come up with an action series that wasn't quite as literal as its spy-thrilling predecessors. Unfortunately, people assume that *The Prisoner* is a sequel to *Secret Agent* because I began the project closely afterward. Number Six is a former "secret agent," which is why people maintain this false notion for the sake of continuity. I would've preferred someone else play the role, but circumstances wouldn't have it that way.

BC: Why'd you decide on the number "6" as a name for your character?

McG: "Six" is the only number which becomes another number when inverted. Turn it upside down and it becomes "9." I like it for that reason. I guess "1" and "0" achieve the same effect, but "6" is far more interesting.

BC: The Village really exists (it's a resort called the Hotel Portmeirion near Cardigan Bay in North Wales). Why'd you decide upon it as a locale?

McG: It's a beautiful place with eight miles of beach. One year I was vacationing there and fell in love with the incredibly diverse forms of architecture; from Mongolian to Portuguese. Just about every type of architecture you could imagine is found there. It was designed by Sir Clough Williams-Ellis, a Welsh gentleman. He did a magnificent job. It's an extraordinary piece of work!

BC: "The Rovers"—the elastic white orbs which track down potential subversives, what do they represent?

McG: The Rovers are the sheepdogs of the allegory. When people start to ask too many questions or assert their individuality, the Rovers act as a stifling force. If one begins to stray from the herd, Rovers are sent out to bring them back. Again, *The Prisoner* is an allegory, enabling me to express this suffocating society in that way.

BC: There were a lot of beautiful women on the show, but you never kissed or romanced any of them. Why?

McG: I didn't think it proper to offend. Nowadays you turn on the television and you see every bloody thing imaginable. I intended upon a family program that children could watch without the sex and all that rubbish.

BC: The show had no other regular characters besides yourself, a silent butler (the dwarf who served Number Two), and Number Two (played by different actors). . . .

McG: Ahh, yesss! Angelo Muscat, a dear fellow, was The Butler. Leo McKern was the only person to play Number Two more than once. He did the character three times; most importantly, he participated in the last two installments which I wrote with him in mind. As for the lead role, again, I would have preferred someone else in it. I would much rather write and direct than act. As a director I'm totally objective. When the film is being edited, I might say, "I don't like the way the actor said that . . . put someone else in the shot." However, the actor that I'm criticizing may very well be me. In that instance I'm not totally objective.

BC: Was the show originally intended to last only one season?

McG: We started out with seven scripts with no intention of expanding it further. Lew Grade wanted twenty-six scripts. I didn't believe the concept could be sustained over that period. We finally did seventeen episodes. Lew Grade read the scripts—(laughing)—he believed that the idea was strange enough to work, so we did them. It's funny, 'cause to this day he doesn't understand what the hell it's all about. He's a hell of a businessman but not that keen from an artistic standpoint.

BC: Are there any further exploits of Number Six, or is he in a retirement home somewhere?

McG: (laughing) No . . . no. The original concept was completely expressed during its television run. We proceeded as planned . . . nothing more . . . nothing less. I'm happy to say that I was pleased with the overall production.

BC: The reason The Prisoner resigns from his post is never revealed within the context of the series. Why did he resign? A hypothetical answer will do.

McG: He simply resigns as a matter of choice. He shouldn't have to answer to anyone. It's entirely his prerogative, his God-given right as an individual, to proceed in any way he sees fit. That's the whole point of it all.

BC: In a statement referring to your character, one of the characters in an episode said, "He can make even the act of putting on his dressing

robe appear as an act of defiance." Number Six was portrayed with a
paranoid yet defiant quality. What made you adhere to that method of
acting?

McG: Paranoid? For God's sake, he wasn't paranoid at all. Is it paranoid
to defend one's right to privacy? As for the method of acting (pause) . . .
I don't think I understand your question.

BC: Let me restate it. Wasn't your character burdened with the circum-
stance of always being watched, causing him to react accordingly . . .
giving his interrogators a disproportionate amount of control; ultimately
inducing paranoia?

McG: If I reserve a seat on a plane and also reserve the seat next to me
so that I won't be bothered by another person's talking, is that paranoia?

BC: I think you've answered my question. The direction and editing of
the series was always consistent, sharp and cutting like the dialogue. How
widespread was your influence over these departments?

McG: I had total control, which is ideal for anyone who wants to accept
that responsibility . . . not blaming anyone else for anything. I picked my
staff. People like Bernard Williams (production manager) and David
Tomblin (producer) were the best in the business. We were able to bring
the project in on schedule and under budget. Each show was about
£54,000. Folks in the business still can't believe we were able to achieve
what we did under that kind of budget. It was the least I could do for
Lew Grade. Hell, the man let me do pretty much what I wanted without
interfering.

BC: Are you interested in creating another television series? Would you
retain the same production staff?

McG: I'm working on a couple of scripts right now, which are not sequels
to *The Prisoner* by any stretch of the imagination, but are extensions of
that theme: the idea of one asserting his rights as an individual.

BC: *Secret Agent* is also being released onto videocassette. You didn't
create the series, but are you receiving proper remuneration for it?

McG: Absolutely! When I did *Secret Agent* and *The Prisoner* I took less
pay than I was initially offered in exchange for a percentage of the profits.
Whoever decided to put the two series on video approached ITC (the
production company), not me. In any event, I am always duly compen-
sated.

BC: John Drake never carried a gun but was one of the more violent
weaponless peacemakers on television. How do you describe his character?

McG: Number Six didn't carry any weapons either. Both characters were able to settle their mutual predicaments by old-fashioned fisticuffs: a much more gentlemanly manner than James Bond's. (Laughing) Your dear President Reagan called James Bond a great symbol for American Freedom . . . for young children to emulate. This is a preposterous idea when you look at the less than ideal manner in which the Bond character conducted himself.

The President has made a lot of miffed statements, but that one is undoubtedly one of the most absurd. I was watching Rich Little the other night on television doing an imitation of him and, let me tell you, it's just not funny anymore. That doting caricature is no longer funny when faced with the realization that you've got four more years of this guy.

BG: Is it true that you refused to divulge the outcome of the final two scripts to even the writers of the previous episodes?

McG: That's correct. I didn't want it to be overanalyzed like everything else, so I revealed the conclusion no sooner than I had to.

I thanked Mr. McGoohan for being surprisingly uninhibited as the interview drew to an end. One facet of his reputation preceded him accurately. He was uncompromising: determined to realize his vision to its fruition. As I left the comfortable ambience of his room (which exuded a hotel suite-ness hauntingly reminiscent of the isolated pseudohomes depicted in *The Prisoner*), he startled me by saying, "We put to rest the final *Prisoner* interview."

PATRICK MCGOOHAN FILMS

It should be noted that McGoohan's acting career did not start before the camera but, instead, on stage. In 1955 he took on one of his more important roles, that of Starbuck in Orson Welles's play *Moby Dick, Rehearsed*. Welles played the role of Ahab. McGoohan continues to perform in the theater to this day.

This filmography was compiled to demonstrate the depth of McGoohan's work in theatrical films. It was often thought that McGoohan didn't have time to make movies, but evidently he did. Unlisted are the many television movies and guest roles in TV shows (one of the most recent being a spot on *Murder, She Wrote*). Some of his best work in television (except, of course, for *Secret Agent* and *The Prisoner*) were two appearances on Peter Falk's *Columbo*, one of which won him an Emmy.

FILMOGRAPHY
Passage Home (Great Britain, 1954)
    McGoohan's first film, a bit part.

Dam Busters (Great Britain, 1955)
    McGoohan played a bit part in this exceptional World War II drama, starring Richard Todd and Michael Redgrave. Directed by Michael Anderson.

I Am a Camera (Great Britain, 1955)
    A small but important role in this film, which was the inspiration for Bob Fosse's *Cabaret*. Controversial at the time and starring Julie Harris, Laurence Harvey, and Shelley Winters. Directed by Henry Cornelius.

The Warriors (Great Britain, 1955)
    Known in the U.K. under the title *The Dark Avenger*, this film is best known as Errol Flynn's last swashbuckler. McGoohan has a small role. Also stars Joanne Dru and Peter Finch. Directed by Henry Levin.

Zarak (Great Britain, 1957)
    Another bit part for McGoohan, this time acting with Victor Mature and Michael Wilding. The location: India. Directed by Terence Young.

High Tide at Noon (Great Britain, 1957)
    McGoohan plays a troublemaker in his first film as a contract player for the Rank Organization.

Hell Drivers (Great Britain, 1958)
    McGoohan has a solid role as Red, the evil force in a labor dispute between management and truckers. Also stars Jill Ireland, Stanley Baker, and two young actors with potential: Sean Connery and David McCallum. Directed by Cy Endfield.

The Gypsy and the Gentleman (Great Britain, 1958)
    McGoohan plays a passionate love interest in this one! A Joseph Losey film full of innuendo and social issues, which also stars Melina Mercouri.

Elephant Gun (Great Britain, 1959)
    Also known as *Moon by Night* and as *Nor the Moon by Night*, McGoohan is cast as one side of a love triangle. Shot in Africa and also starring Belinda Lee and Michael Craig. Directed by Ken Annakin.

All Night Long (Great Britain, 1961)

An updating of *Othello*, with McGoohan playing Iago's role as a jazz drummer. (Possibly the inspiration for "Hammer into Anvil"?) Also features Richard Attenborough and musical appearances by Dave Brubeck, Charlie Mingus, and John Dankworth. Directed by Basil Dearden.

Two Living, One Dead (Sweden, 1961)

Directed by Anthony Asquith, McGoohan plays the role of a bank teller who must deal with various accusations after a robbery attempt.

Walk in the Shadow (Great Britain, 1962)

Also released as *Life for Ruth* and as *No Life for Ruth*. McGoohan plays a doctor dealing with the theme of the individual versus society. With Janet Munro and Paul Rogers and directed by Basil Dearden.

The Quare Fellow (Ireland, 1962)

Solid adaptation of a Brendan Behan play, with McGoohan cast as a prison guard who wrestles with the idea of capital punishment. Also stars Sylvia Syms and Walter Macken. Directed by Arthur Dreifuss.

The Three Lives of Thomasina (United States, 1964)

Disney film about a cat, directed by one of McGoohan's *Prisoner* cohorts, Don Chaffey. Lead role for McGoohan as veterinarian.

Ice Station Zebra (United States, 1967)

Based on the Alistair MacLean novel, McGoohan plays a familiar role: a British secret agent out to subvert Russian intelligence. Also stars Rock Hudson, Ernest Borgnine, and Jim Brown. Directed by John Sturges.

The Moonshine War (United States, 1970)

Revenue agent McGoohan is out to ensnare some bootleggers just before the repeal of Prohibition. Also starring Alan Alda. Directed by Richard Quine.

Mary, Queen of Scots (Great Britain, 1971)

McGoohan plays James Stuart in this historic costume drama, which also featured Vanessa Redgrave, Timothy Dalton, and Glenda Jackson. Directed by Charles Jarrott.

Catch My Soul (United States, 1974)

Also known as *Santa Fe Satan*, this film—which is directed by but does not star McGoohan—is a rock 'n' roll version of *Othello*, with Richie Havens, Tony Joe White, and Susan Tyrrell.

Silver Streak (United States, 1976)

This was the most successful teaming of Richard Pryor and Gene Wilder. McGoohan plays an art-forging villain. Directed by Arthur Hiller.

Kings and Desperate Men (Great Britain, 1977)

Directed by The Kid, Alexis Kanner, and dealing with some very *Prisoner*esque themes.

Brass Target (United States, 1978)

McGoohan joins plenty of heavyweight actors—John Cassavetes, Sophia Loren, George Kennedy, Max von Sydow—in this speculation about the assassination of General George Patton. Directed by John Hough.

Escape from Alcatraz (United States, 1979)

McGoohan plays the role of warden with relish in this kind-of-based-on-fact thriller starring Clint Eastwood. Directed by Donald Siegel.

Scanners (United States, 1981)

Directed by David Cronenberg, a very cerebral horror film, with McGoohan well cast as a man who has perverted science.

Baby . . . Secret of the Lost Legend (United States, 1985)

Offbeat film about a baby dinosaur adopted by a young couple. McGoohan doesn't appear to be very involved in his role.

APPENDIX A:

SOURCES OF INFORMATION

ORGANIZATIONS

At any given time there are dozens of different fanzines, clubs, and special interest groups devoted to the study or appreciation of *The Prisoner*. However, only two of those groups—The Six of One and Once Upon a Time—have demonstrated the ability to maintain, persist, and overcome coercion. Both publish regular newsletters and magazines and are good sources of information.

THE SIX OF ONE

This is the oldest and most established group, based in Ipswich. The group, which addresses itself as The Prisoner Appreciation Society, was officially founded on January 6, 1977, and takes its name from a popular phrase used often in *The Prisoner*: Six of one; half a dozen of the other. The fact that six and one are both mentioned in this phrase can be read as another clue to the true identity of Number Six—which is Number One. Patrick McGoohan is the honorary chairman of this group. Its membership, in the thousands, is worldwide.

The organization publishes a quarterly magazine of high standards, entitled *Number Six*. The magazine is sent to members of the society, who also receive periodic information on the society's activities. The Six of One makes much *Prisoner* memorabilia available for purchase, and it organizes a yearly convention at the Hotel Portmeirion in North Wales (discussed later).

Much of the hard scholarship on *The Prisoner* has been conducted by members of this society. It was through their efforts that "The Alternate Chimes of Big Ben" was discovered. To become a member (or to get more information), contact:

(IN THE U.K.)   *(IN THE UNITED STATES)*

SIX OF ONE   SIX OF ONE
P.O. Box 66   P.O. Box 172
Ipswich IP2 9TZ   Hatfield, PA 19440
ENGLAND

ONCE UPON A TIME
Nine years old and still going strong, Once Upon a Time is a nonprofit fan club "for all those who appreciate *The Prisoner*." Members of the organization are entitled to three copies of the low-budget but thoughtful club magazine, an episode guide, a map of The Village, a copy of the *Tally Ho*, and access to the library of books, articles, documents, and newsletters on *The Prisoner* (free ten-day loan). Once Upon a Time also maintains a databank of special-interest groups on *The Prisoner*, ranging from those who write fiction to those who actively follow the career of Patrick McGoohan. If there is a special focus to this society, it is the emphasis on "creeping bureaucracy and restrictions of freedom."

For membership information, write to:

ONCE UPON A TIME
515 Ravenel Circle
Seneca, SC 29678

BOOKS ON *THE PRISONER*
There have been many interesting books published on *The Prisoner*. Although many of them are out of print, they can be borrowed from places like the lending library of Once Upon a Time. If they are in print, they can be purchased through The Six of One club.

PORTMEIRION PRISONER PRODUCTION
Compiled by Max Hora (A Number Six Publication, 1985)
This 28-page book provides a day-to-day account of *The Prisoner*'s production at Portmeirion in September of 1966. It also provides information on the debate of proper screening orders.

THE MAKING OF *THE PRISONER*
by Roger Langley (Escape Publications, 1985)
A 24-page book that offers a new look into the production of the show. The book provides much information on the creative decision-making and on how the budget affected the final series.

THINK TANK
by Roger Langley (Escape Publications, 1984)
A novel based on The Prisoner.

VILLAGE WORLD
by Max Hora (Six of One, 1987)
A series of essays and insights into miscellaneous aspects of *The Prisoner*. Includes much location information (such as where the real chessboard is) and 66 interesting observations and facts.

THE PRISONER SHOP

On the grounds of the Portmeirion Village Hotel is The Prisoner Shop, run by The Six of One. If you're interested in stationery, posters, photographs, Village maps, candles, buttons, pens, and other paraphernalia related to *The Prisoner*, this is the place to shop. Address your inquiries to:

THE PRISONER SHOP
Portmeirion Village Hotel
Penrhyndeudraeth
Gwynedd LL48 6ER
WALES

ANNUAL PORTMEIRION CONVENTION
Every summer Six of One organizes a convention at Portmeirion, the real location of The Village. The three-day program has become a "must" for hard-core *Prisoner* fans. Tours of the grounds provide much insight into The Village. A game of human chess can be played on the same spot where it was played in "Checkmate." Participants in the making of *The Prisoner* are often on hand to answer questions. Other activities include special screenings of episodes, discussion groups, and theater exercises based on *The Prisoner*. Many people come fully dressed as Villagers or as Number Six himself. If this sounds like your idea of a summer vacation, contact Six of One at the address given previously.

ITC ENTERTAINMENT LIMITED

ITC is the production company that funded the making of the series and owns the commercial rights. If you want to copy a photograph, or if you have a script idea based on *The Prisoner*, talk with them first. They can be reached in both the U.K. and the United States:

(IN THE U.K.)

ITC ENTERTAINMENT LIMITED
Cullum House
North Orbital Road
Denham, Uxbridge
Middlesex UB9 5HL
ENGLAND

(IN THE UNITED STATES)

ITC ENTERTAINMENT LIMITED
115 East 57th Street
New York, NY 10022

MPI HOME VIDEO

MPI home video distributes *The Prisoner* throughout the United States. For ordering information, contact them at:

MPI HOME VIDEO
15825 Rob Roy Drive
Oak Forest, IL 60452
1-800-323-0442

APPENDIX B:

THE
SHOOTING
SCRIPTS

Reprinted here are some excerpts from the original shooting scripts of *The Prisoner*. It is important to note that what appears in the scripts is not necessarily what appears on screen. Often, an actor would improvise a scene on the set, the director or McGoohan would like it, and that improvised scene would replace the scripted scene. Also, many scenes were cut or altered in the editing room—either for time considerations or for creative ones. And there were several instances where an episode was shot according to the shooting script and then, after viewing, was reshot under new directions.

Although these shooting scripts may not reflect the exact activity on the screen, they do offer us valuable insights into the making of *The Prisoner*. These were, after all, the documents by which cast and crew combined their efforts to create the show. Within this section are excerpts from many of the most celebrated moments of the series.

There are a few things to keep in mind when reading the scripts. Number Six, the part played by Patrick McGoohan, is always referred to as "P" in the shooting scripts (which could stand for either Prisoner or Patrick). The numbers that appear at the right-hand side of the page indicate changes in location or a special camera move. These numbers help the crew organize the shots by location, and much of the locations are described in a type of shorthand. "INT" stands for an *interior shot* (for example, inside The Green Dome). "EXT" stands for *exterior shot* (as in outside The Green Dome). "EST" stands for *establishing shot* (if action is going to take place on the beach, a shot that establishes the beach in the viewer's mind would be called for). "LOC" stands for *location*, and represents those scenes that must be shot at Portmeirion and not, for example, in a studio. "P.O.V." stands for *point of view*. The rest of the notes should be self-explanatory.

The Opening Sequence
From "ARRIVAL"

STANDARD OPENING

FADE IN:

STORM CLOUDS. DAY. (STOCK)   A

BLACK. MENACING. A CRASH OF THUNDER. JAGGED FLARE OF LIGHTNING. MORE THUNDER MERGING INTO THE HIGH-PITCHED SCREAM OF A JET AIRCRAFT.

MIX FAST TO:

EXT. AERODROME. DAY. LOC.   B

A VAST DESERTED RUNWAY STRETCHING INTO THE DISTANCE. THE JET SCREAM FADES TO ABSOLUTE SILENCE. A TINY SPECK HURTLING AT WHAT APPEARS TO BE SUPERSONIC SPEED TOWARDS CAMERA. IT IS A SILVER LOTUS 7. IT EXPLODES INTO LENS WITH THE CRACK OF THE SOUND BARRIER BEING BROKEN.

SHOCK CUT TO:

INT. LOTUS 7. DAY. LOC.   C

P DRIVING. HIS FACE TAUT AGAINST WIND PRESSURE. HIS HAIR SWEPT BACK BY SLIP-STREAM. HIS EXPRESSION GRIM.

EXT. LONDON. DAY. LOC.   D

WE SEE THE PANORAMA OF LONDON BELOW AND ZOOM IN TO PICK OUT THE ANT-LIKE LOTUS 7, DARTING ANGRILY THROUGH TRAFFIC.

EXT. UNDERGROUND GARAGE. DAY. LOC.   E

A DOUBLE-DECKER LONDON TRANSPORT BUS COMES LUMBERING TOWARDS US. THE LOTUS EMERGES FROM BEHIND IT, OVERTAKES AND SWERVES ACROSS THE FRONT TO DISAPPEAR DOWN INTO THE BOWELS OF AN UNDERGROUND GARAGE.

INT. UNDERGROUND LIFT SHAFT. DAY.   F

SHOOTING UP, THE LIFT DROPS LIKE A STONE. IT STOPS AND P GETS
OUT. WE PAN WITH HIM AS HE WALKS FAST IN DETERMINATION
DOWN A LONG CORRIDOR.

INT. LONG CORRIDOR. DAY.   G

HOLDING P VERY LARGE WE TRACK BACK. HE GOES IN AND OUT OF
POOLS OF LIGHT. HE OVERTAKES US AND WE PAN WITH HIM TO
SHOW THE REST OF THE CORRIDOR. HE CRASHES THROUGH A DOOR
AT THE END. WE SEE A MAN SITTING AT A DESK. HE IS FORMALLY
DRESSED. BUREAUCRATIC. THE OFFICE IS PAINTED WHITE. IN LONG
SHOT WE SEE P FORCEFULLY PACING. HE IS GESTICULATING ANGRILY.
THE LANGUAGE WOULD BE STRONG IF WE COULD HEAR WHAT IS
BEING SAID. WE CAN'T. INSTEAD EACH DYNAMIC GESTURE IS PUNC-
TUATED BY A CLAP OF THUNDER. THE OTHER MAN IS STILL AND
THOUGHTFUL. HE SAYS NOTHING. P TAKES AN ENVELOPE FROM HIS
POCKET AND THROWS IT ON THE DESK. HE SLAMS OUT.

INT. COMPUTER RECORD ROOM. DAY.   H

WITH EXAGGERATED METALLIC SOUND A COMPUTER FLICKS RAPIDLY
THROUGH A STACK OF RECORDER CARDS. ONE CARD DROPS OUT
ONTO A MOVING FEEDER BELT. WE SEE ON IT A PHOTOGRAPH OF
P.

INT. FILING ROOM. DAY.   I

A PERSPECTIVE OF FILING CABINETS. SEEMINGLY ENDLESS. WE MOVE
FAST ALONG IT. A DRAWER OPENS OF ITS OWN VOLITION. THE PRIS-
ONER'S CARD IS DROPPED IN. THE DRAWER SNAPS SHUT. ZOOM IN
TO THE ONE WORD ON THE CABINET LABEL—RESIGNED.

EXT. P'S LONDON HOME. DAY. LOC.   J

HE DRIVES UP IN THE LOTUS. STOPS. GETS OUT. UNLOCKS THE FRONT
DOOR AND ENTERS. PAN OFF TO SEE THE DISTANT FIGURE OF A MAN
GIVING A SIGNAL.

INT. BEDROOM OF P'S LONDON HOME. DAY.   K

HE IS PACKING IN SOME HURRY. HE CHECKS HIS WATCH. HE APPEARS
TO HAVE A WEIGHT OFF HIS MIND. IN EVIDENCE, A HOLIDAY BRO-
CHURE AND AN AIR TICKET.

EXT. P'S LONDON HOME. DAY. LOC.   L

A HEARSE PULLS UP. FOUR MEN IN PROPER ATTIRE GET OUT AND
MOVE PURPOSEFULLY TO THE FRONT DOOR.

INT. DEN OF P'S LONDON HOME. DAY.   M

PACKED SUITCASE. THE AIR TICKET GOES INTO A POCKET. THE DOOR-
BELL PEALS. HE MOVES TO THE WINDOW AND LOOKS OUT.

HIS P.O.V. LOC.   N

THE STANDARD LONDON SCENE. SUN SHINES BRIGHTLY.

INT. DEN OF P'S LONDON HOME. DAY.   O

HE DROPS THE VENETIAN BLIND AGAINST THE GLARE. HE TURNS TO
ANSWER THE DOOR. HE IS POLE-AXED IN SHOCK. HIS EYES GO. HE
GRABS AT HIS THROAT. HE STAGGERS AND FALLS ONTO THE DIVAN
BESIDE THE WINDOW. WHIP-PAN ACROSS TO THE KEYHOLE OF THE
DOOR TO THE ROOM. A JET OF VAPOUR HISSES THROUGH.

MIX FAST TO:

EXT. LONDON. DAY. (HELICOPTER SHOT). LOC.   P

CAMERA MOVING AWAY. THE LONDON SCENE IS FAST DISAPPEARING
BELOW.

EXT. COASTLINE. DAY. (HELICOPTER SHOT). LOC.   Q

CAMERA MOVING IN. BENEATH IS SEA AND A PENINSULA OF LAND.
NO DETAIL. APPROACHING FAST. ZOOM TO OUT-OF-FOCUS. PULL
BACK TO:

INT. P'S ROOM. DAY.   R

CLOSE UP OF P. GROGGY. HE COMES TO. HE RISES AND MOVES TO
THE WINDOW FOR SOME AIR. HE PULLS THE VENETIAN BLIND AND
LOOKS OUT.

EXT. THE VILLAGE. DAY. LOC.   S

HIS P.O.V.—IN PLACE OF THE ESTABLISHED LONDON VIEW WE HAVE
A PANORAMA OF THE VILLAGE OF PORTMEIRION.

EXT. WINDOW OF P'S ROOM. DAY. LOC.   T

P STANDING AT THE WINDOW. IN SHOCK.

FREEZE FRAME

MAIN TITLES

N.B. THE STANDARD OPENING WILL BE SHOT AND PERFORMED AT
GREAT SPEED. IT WILL BE OPTICALLY STYLISED. MAIN TITLES WILL
BE RUN OVER GEOGRAPHICAL STILLS OF THE VILLAGE AND ITS
ESSENTIAL COMPONENTS.

The First Encounters in The Village
From "ARRIVAL"

FADE IN

ACT ONE

INT. PRISONER'S ROOM. DAY.   1

THE PRISONER STANDS AT THE WINDOW AND STARES OUT. HE TURNS
AND LOOKS AROUND. THE ROOM IS IDENTICAL TO THE ONE IN HIS
LONDON RESIDENCE—SAME DIVAN, SAME CARPET, SAME WALL PAPER,
THE SAME PICTURE ON THE WALL. HE RUSHES TO THE DOOR.

EXT. HOUSE AND STREET. DAY. LOC.   2

HE BURSTS OUT

EXT. THE VILLAGE. DAY. LOC.   3

P.O.V. OF THE SILENT EMPTY VILLAGE

EXT. P'S HOUSE AND STREET. DAY. LOC.   4

A CLOSE-SHOT OF P. HE LOOKS UP.

EXT. BALCONY BY BELL TOWER. DAY. LOC.   5

THE FIGURE OF A MAN IN SILHOUETTE LOOKING DOWN.

EXT. P'S HOUSE AND STREET. DAY. LOC.   6

P RUNS UP THE STEPS TOWARD THE WATCHER.

EXT. STEPS. DAY. LOC.   7

SHOOTING DOWN, WE SEE P RUSH TOWARDS US.

EXT. THE BALCONY. DAY. LOC.   8

HE APPEARS VERY LARGE IN CAMERA AND WE PAN HIM TO INCLUDE
THE WATCHER IN FOREGROUND. THE WATCHER IS A STONE STATUE.
P LOOKS DOWNWARDS.

EXT. SEA AND VILLAGE FORESHORE. DAY. LOC.   9

HIS P.O.V. THE STILLNESS OF THE VILLAGE IS ACCENTUATED BY THE
SEA BEYOND

EXT. THE BALCONY. DAY. LOC.   10

HE HEARS A SUDDEN GRATING SOUND AND RUNS TO A VANTAGE
POINT.

EXT. CAFE. DAY. LOC.   11

LONG P.O.V. OF FIGURE MOVING AMONG TABLES AND CHAIRS OF
OPEN AIR CAFE.

EXT. VANTAGE POINT. DAY. LOC.   12

P. WE PAN HIM AS HE HURRIES TOWARDS THE CAFE.

EXT. CAFE FORECOURT. DAY. LOC.   13

HE COMES UP AND STOPS BY A TABLE. CUT TO THE FIGURE HE HAS
SEEN—A WAITRESS GETTING THE PLACE READY FOR BUSINESS. SHE
IS MIDDLE-AGED.

WAITRESS
We'll be open in a minute.

P
What's the name of this place?

WAITRESS
You're new here, aren't you?

P
Where?

WAITRESS
You want breakfast?

P
Where is this?

WAITRESS
The village?

                              P
Yes.

                         WAITRESS
I'll see if coffee's ready.

                              P
Where's the police station?

                         WAITRESS
There isn't one.

                              P
Can I use your phone?

                         WAITRESS
We haven't got one.

                              P
Where can I make a call?

                         WAITRESS
Phone box round the corner.
Breakfast won't be a minute.

HE MOVES OFF. WAITRESS LOOKS AFTER HIM, RESUMES HER CHORES.

EXT. PHONE BOX. DAY. LOC.   14

IT IS A TELEPHONE BOOTH NOT UNFAMILIAR BUT NOT EXACTLY LIKE
THE ONES WE ARE USED TO. P ENTERS IT.

INT. PHONE BOX. DAY.   15

MODERN STYLE TELEPHONE BUT WITHOUT COIN BOX.
THE DIAL IS WITHOUT NUMBERS OR LETTERS OR EXCHANGE DISC.

INT. PHONE BOX. DAY.   16

HE PICKS UP THE PHONE.

                    GIRL OPERATOR'S VOICE
Number please?

                              P
What exchange is this?

                     OPERATOR'S VOICE
Number please.

                              P
I want to make a call.

> OPERATOR'S VOICE
> (STILL CORRECT BUT LOSING
> PATIENCE) Local calls only.
> What is your number, sir?
>
> P
> (LOOKING AT THE BLANK
> DIAL) I haven't got a number.
>
> OPERATOR'S VOICE
> No number. No call.

HE IS DISCONNECTED. HE TRIES TO GET THROUGH AGAIN. HE JIG-
GLES THE PHONE REST UP AND DOWN. THERE IS NO REACTION. THE
PHONE IS DEAD. HE LEAVES THE BOOTH.

EXT. A STREET. DAY. LOC.   17

HE SEES AN ARROWED SIGN SAYING "TAXI" AND FOLLOWS ITS DI-
RECTION

EXT. TAXI RANK. DAY. LOC.   18

THREE MINI-MOKE "BEACH BUGGIES" ARE PARKED IN LINE. THE
"BUGGIES" HAVE ORNAMENTAL CANVAS ROOFS AND ARE CLEARLY
MARKED "TAXI." THERE ARE NO DRIVERS TO BE SEEN. HE PRESSES
THE HORN OF THE FIRST "BUGGY" AND LOOKS AROUND, WAITING.

> GIRL'S VOICE
> (PERFECT ENGLISH)
> Where to, sir?
>
> GIRL DRIVER
> (FRENCH)
> Where do you want to go?
>
> P
> The nearest town.
>
> GIRL DRIVER
> (LOOKS AT HIM FOR A MO-
> MENT)
> Oh! We're only a local service.

PRISONER REACTS TO "LOCAL"

> P
> Take me as far as you can.

THE GIRL GIVES ANOTHER STRANGE LOOK. THEY GET INTO THE
"BUGGY." SHE DRIVES OFF.

EXT. VARIOUS STREETS AND ASPECTS OF VILLAGE. DAY. LOC.   19

VARIOUS SHOTS DRIVING THROUGH WINDING LANES, FOREST PATHS, VILLAGE SQUARES, ETC. THE PRISONER TAKES IN HIS FIRST EXTENDED VIEW OF THE VILLAGE ON GROUND LEVEL.

INT. "BUGGY." DAY. LOC.   20

P TURNS TO THE GIRL DRIVER.

> P
>
> Why did you speak to me in French?

> GIRL DRIVER
> (WITHOUT TURNING HER HEAD)
> French is international.

> P
>
> I suppose it's a waste of time to ask the name of this place?

> GIRL DRIVER
> As a matter of fact, I thought you might be Polish. Maybe Czech.

> P
>
> What would Poles and Czechs be doing here?

> GIRL DRIVER
> It's very cosmopolitan. You never know who you meet next.

> P
>
> Why do you keep avoiding my questions?

> GIRL DRIVER
> Do I?

SHE LOOKS IN THE DRIVING MIRROR AT HIM.

EXT. VILLAGE AND ENVIRONS. DAY. LOC.   21

WE SEE MORE OF DIFFERENT VIEWS AND ASPECTS OF THE VILLAGE.

INT. "BUGGY" DAY. LOC.   22

                      P
This is an unusual job for a girl.

              GIRL DRIVER
Driving a cab? I don't see why.

                      P
First time I've seen a cab like
this.

              GIRL DRIVER
We've got several. They're very
handy.

P. CLOSE SHOT. REACTING TO WHAT HE SEES.

EXT. VILLAGE. DAY. LOC.   23

HIS P.O.V. HE IS BACK IN THE VILLAGE MORE OR LESS WHERE HE
STARTED FROM. THE CAB HAS STOPPED.

INT. "BUGGY". DAY. LOC.   24

P GIVES THE GIRL A PUZZLED LOOK.

              GIRL DRIVER
I did tell you we're only local.

HE IS NOW FIGURING IT OUT.

              GIRL DRIVER
The charge is two units. Money
tokens.

HE GETS OUT.

              GIRL DRIVER
Oh well, pay me next time.

SHE SMILES AND GIVES AN ODD WAVE OF THE HAND. IT COULD
ALMOST BE A SALUTE.

              GIRL DRIVER
Be seeing you.

SHE DRIVES OFF LEAVING HIM STANDING IN THE VILLAGE STREET.

EXT. BATTERY SQUARE. DAY. LOC.   25

CLOSE SHOT OF P TAKING STOCK. HE IS AWARE THAT SOMETHING
VERY STRANGE IS GOING ON. HE SEES A GENERAL STORE IN FRONT
OF HIM. HE GOES IN. THE DOOR-BELL RINGS.

INT. GENERAL STORE. DAY.   26

AS HE ENTERS, THE SHOPKEEPER, AN ELDERLY MAN IS JUST FINISHING
SERVING A CUSTOMER. THE SHOPKEEPER IS SAYING SOMETHING IN
A FOREIGN LANGUAGE BUT AS SOON AS HE SEES P HE STOPS.

>   SHOPKEEPER
>   (BREAKING INTO ENGLISH)
>   Well, good day then. *Be seeing
>   you.*

THE CUSTOMER, CLUTCHING A PINEAPPLE, LEAVES THE SHOP GIVING
P A SLIGHT GLANCE AS HE PASSES.

>   SHOPKEEPER
>   (VERY PLEASANT)
>   And what can I do for you, sir?

>   P
>   I want a map. A map of this area.

>   SHOPKEEPER
>   Colour, or black and white?

>   P
>   Just show me a map.

THE SHOPKEEPER MOVES AROUND, LOOKING THROUGH THE SHELVES.
PERHAPS OPENING A DRAWER OR TWO.

>   SHOPKEEPER
>   (MUTTERING TO HIMSELF)
>   Let's see. Black and white. Ah
>   —I thought so.

HE FISHES OUT A SMALL FOLDED MAP FROM A STACK BEHIND TINS
OF BAKED BEANS.

>   SHOPKEEPER
>   Here we are. Shows you every-
>   thing.

THE PRISONER UNFOLDS THE MAP AND SPREADS IT OUT ON THE
COUNTER.

IT SHOWS THE VILLAGE AND THE PENINSULA ON WHICH IT STANDS,
WITH THE MOUNTAINS AND THE FOREST FORMING NATURAL BOUND-
ARIES. THERE ARE NO PLACE NAMES. EVERYTHING IS MERELY "THE
SEA", "THE MOUNTAINS", "THE BEACH".

P

I meant a larger map.

SHOPKEEPER

Only in colour. More expensive.

P

Yes, yes.

THE SHOPKEEPER BENDS DOWN AND FROM UNDER THE COUNTER
HE PRODUCES A MUCH LARGER MAP IN A FOLDER. P SPREADS IT ON
TOP OF THE SMALLER ONE.

THIS IS ESSENTIALLY THE SAME, BUT IN COLOUR. THERE IS MORE
DETAIL, SHOWING INDIVIDUAL BUILDINGS IN THE VILLAGE WHICH
HAVE MARKINGS LIKE "LABOUR EXCHANGE", "PALACE OF FUN",
"COUNCIL OFFICES", "CITIZEN'S ADVICE BUREAU". BUT AGAIN THERE
ARE NO PLACE NAMES. IT IS STILL ONLY "THE SEA", ETC.

P

This isn't what I meant. I meant
a bigger area.

SHOPKEEPER

We only have local maps.
There's no demand for any oth-
ers.
(BEAT)
You're new here, aren't you?

FOR A MOMENT THEY LOOK AT EACH OTHER. THERE IS NO NEED
TO SAY ANYMORE.

P

Where can I hire a car? Self-
drive.

SHOPKEEPER

No self-drive here. Only taxis.

P

I've tried those.

THE SHOP BELL RINGS. A WOMAN CUSTOMER, VERY MUCH THE
HOUSEWIFE, COMES IN AND GOES STRAIGHT TO THE COUNTER. P
MOVES TO LEAVE THE SHOP. THE SHOPKEEPER CALLS:

SHOPKEEPER

I hope I'll have your custom,
sir.

HE SMILES AND GIVES AN ODD WAVE OF THE HAND. IT COULD ALMOST BE A SALUTE.

                              SHOPKEEPER
                    Be seeing you.

P, HAVING HEARD IT THREE TIMES NOW, REACTS TO "BE SEEING YOU" AS HE LEAVES.

EXT. BATTERY SQUARE. DAY. LOC.   27

HE EMERGES FROM THE SHOP. HE SEES A PUSH BUTTON ELECTRIC INDICATOR BOARD WITH THE INSCRIPTION "INFORMATION BOARD". HE GOES UP TO IT AND FINDS IT IS AN ELECTRICALLY OPERATED MAP OF THE VILLAGE SHOWING KEY BUILDINGS AND FACILITIES. HE PUSHES A BUTTON MARKED "TRANSPORT" AND AN ARROW LIGHTS UP INDICATING "TAXI". HE PUSHES OTHER BUTTONS IN TURN AND THEY LIGHT UP THE VARIOUS LOCATIONS ON THE MAP. SUDDENLY HE HEARS O.S. A MECHANICALLY CHEERFUL VOICE A LA DISC JOCKEY.

                              VOICE O.S.
                    (BUBBLING   WITH   AUTO-
                    MATED ZEST)
                    Good morning, all. It's another
                    beautiful day.

THE VOICE IS COMING FROM LOUDSPEAKERS DOTTED ROUND THE VILLAGE AND FROM THOSE LOUDSPEAKERS NOW COMES LIVELY BUT NOT INTRUSIVE MUSIC, ONE OR TWO PEOPLE BEGIN TO APPEAR IN THE DISTANCE. THE VILLAGE IS SLOWLY COMING TO LIFE.

BUT THE PRISONER IS INTERESTED IN SOMETHING ELSE. OPPOSITE IS THE HOUSE WHERE HE WOKE UP. IN THE WINDOW OF HIS ROOM HE CATCHES A GLIMPSE OF A YOUNG WOMAN BLONDE AND AT-TRACTIVE. SHE GOES OUT OF SIGHT.

EXT. P'S HOUSE AND STREET. DAY. LOC.   28

HE RUNS TO THE HOUSE. THIS IS THE FIRST TIME WE NOTICE THERE IS A NUMBER ON THE DOOR—NUMBER SIX. THE DOOR HAS NO LOCK.

INT. P'S ROOM. DAY.   29

HE ENTERS. THERE IS NO ONE THERE. BUT THERE HAVE BEEN CHANGES. THERE IS NOW A TELEVISION SET BY THE WALL, AND A VERY MODERN LOOKING TELEPHONE WITH NUMBER SIX ON THE DIAL BY THE DI-VAN. THERE IS A VASE OF FLOWERS ON A TABLE AND A CARD WITH A MESSAGE. THERE IS ALSO THE BACKGROUND OF MOOD MUSIC.

INSERT OF CARD:

"WELCOME TO YOUR HOME FROM HOME"

HE TAKES IN ALL THIS BUT IS MORE CONCERNED ABOUT FINDING THE STRANGE GIRL HE SAW IN THE WINDOW. HE HEARS THE DOOR SLAM. HE GOES TO THE WINDOW AND SEES THE RATHER PLEASING BACKVIEW OF THE GIRL FROM THE HOUSE. HE IS ABOUT TO FOLLOW HER WHEN THE PHONE RINGS. HE GRABS THE RECEIVER.

> GIRL OPERATOR'S VOICE
> Is your number six?

> P
> (LOOKING AT THE WALL)
> Yes.

> GIRL OPERATOR'S VOICE
> Just one moment. I have a call
> for you.

ACT TWO

FADE IN:
EXT. GEORGIAN HOUSE AND APPROACH. DAY. LOC.   31

TWO MEN WORKING IN THE GARDENS OF THE GEORGIAN HOUSE. THE FIGURE OF THE PRISONER ENTERS FOREGROUND. HE STARTS TO WALK UP THE LONG GARDEN PATH TOWARDS THE HOUSE. HE LOOKS AT THE GARDENERS. THEY APPARENTLY DON'T NOTICE HIM.

EXT. GEORGIAN HOUSE AND APPROACH. DAY. LOC.   32

P COMES UP THE PATH AND WE PAN HIM TO THE ORNATE FRONT DOOR. IT BEARS THE NUMBER TWO. THERE IS A BELL CHAIN WHICH HE PULLS. THE OLD-FASHIONED BELL TINKLES IN THE DEPTH OF THE HOUSE. CLOSE-UP OF P LOOKING AROUND WHILE HE WAITS. THE DOOR IS OPENED TO REVEAL A BUTLER. HE IS VERY FORMAL BUT A MAN IN OBVIOUSLY GOOD PHYSICAL SHAPE WHO'D BE AT HOME IN AN E-TYPE JAG.

> BUTLER
> Ah, yes. This way, sir.

INT. ANTE ROOM. DAY.   33

THIS SET IS DRESSED IN CHARACTER WITH THE EXTERIOR OF THE HOUSE. THERE IS ONE CENTRAL DOOR LEADING OFF IT. THE BUTLER, LEADING THE WAY, OPENS THIS DOOR TO DISCLOSE:

INT. LIVING SPACE. DAY.   34

THE LIVING SPACE TAKES UP THE ENTIRE GROUND OF THE HOUSE.
IT IS A HIGHLY STYLISED SET. FUTURISTIC. THERE IS A FEELING OF
VAST, ALMOST UNENDING SPACE. IN THE CENTRE AT A HALF-MOON
DESK WE SEE NUMBER 2, THE CHAIRMAN OF THE VILLAGE. THERE IS
NO OTHER FURNITURE. HE IS ABOUT 45, INTELLECTUAL, HANDSOME
AND DANGEROUSLY CHARMING.

>   NO. 2
>   At last. Delighted to see you.
>   Come in, come in.

P TAKES THE LONG WALK TO THE DESK.

>   NO. 2
>   Do sit down.

BUT THERE IS NO CHAIR. NO. 2 BEAMS AND PUSHES A BUTTON. A
BUZZING SOUND AS A CHAIR EMERGES FROM THE FLOOR ON THE
RIGHT OF NO. 2.

>   NO. 2
>   I'm so sorry. I can never resist
>   that.

HE SWIVELS TO HIS RIGHT TO FACE THE OTHER CHAIR AS P SITS
DOWN. NO. 2 PUSHES ANOTHER BUTTON ON HIS CHAIR CONSOLE
AND A DINING TABLE MATERIALISES BETWEEN THEM. THE BUTLER
APPEARS PUSHING A TROLLEY. HE STARTS TO LAY OUT BREAKFAST
WHILE THEY SPEAK.

>   NO. 2
>   You don't mind a working
>   breakfast? Tea or coffee?

>   P
>   Tea.

>   NO. 2
>   Indian or China?

>   P
>   Either—with lemon.

>   NO. 2
>   (TO THE BUTLER)
>   That'll be all.

THE BUTLER LEAVES. NO. 2 GETS UP AND STARTS SERVING BREAKFAST
FROM THE TROLLEY.

NO. 2
Two eggs with your bacon?

P DOES NOT ANSWER.

NO. 2
I suppose you're wondering
what you're doing here?

P
(DANGEROUSLY)
It had crossed my mind.

NO. 2
Help yourself to toast.

AS NO. 2 SITS DOWN AT THE TABLE, P GETS UP AND WALKS AROUND
THE TABLE TO HIM, A TIME BOMB ABOUT TO EXPLODE.

P
Right. What's it all about?

THEY HOLD A LOOK FOR A MOMENT. THEN NO. 2 PUSHES A BUTTON
ON HIS CHAIR CONSOLE AND BEHIND P FROM THE FLOOR EMERGES
A BLACK LEATHER SWIVEL ARMCHAIR.

NO. 2
Sit down and I'll tell you.

P REMAINS STANDING.

NO. 2
It's the question of your retirement.

P
Go on.

NO. 2
The information in your head
is priceless. I don't think you
realise what a valuable property you have become. A man
like you is in great demand on
the open market.

P
Who brought me here?

NO. 2
I know exactly how you feel,
believe me. They have taken
quite a liberty.

P
And who are they?

NO. 2
A lot of people are curious about
what lies behind your resignation. You've had a brilliant career. Your record is impeccable.
They want to know why you
suddenly left.

P
What people?

NO. 2
Personally, I believe your story.
I think it really was a matter of
principle. But what I think
doesn't really count. One has to
be sure about these things.

P
That gives you the right to poke
your nose into my business?

NO. 2
Please. It is my job to check your
motive.

P
I've been checked.

NO. 2
Of course. But when a man
knows as much as you do, a
double check does no harm. A
few details may have been
missed.

P
I don't know who you are or
who you work for and I don't
care. I'm leaving.

P IS ON THE MOVE, GOING TOWARDS THE DOOR.

INT. LIVING SPACE. DAY.   35

P REACHES THE DOOR TO FIND IT IS FLUSH FITTING WITH NO HAN-
DLE.

NO. 2
Have you not yet realised there
is no way out? Look, I have
something that will interest you.

BEHIND NO. 2, A SECTION OF THE WALL HAS BECOME TRANSLUCENT.
HE HAS A FILE IN HIS HAND. HE OPENS THE FOLDER TO PAGE ONE.
A PICTURE OF A BABY APPEARS ON THE TRANSLUCENT SCREEN. NO.
2 TURNS ANOTHER PAGE AND SIMULTANEOUSLY THE PICTURE
CHANGES. IT IS NOW A SMALL BOY IN SCHOOL UNIFORM. P ADVANCES
DOWN THE ROOM AND LOOKS AT HIS FILE OVER NO. 2'S SHOULDER.
AS EACH PAGE IS TURNED, THE PICTURE CHANGES. WE SEE P IN
VARIOUS STAGES OF HIS DEVELOPMENT. P SNATCHES THE FILE.

NO. 2
Feel free.

P STARTS TO TURN THE PAGES WITH INCREASING SPEED. AS HE DOES
SO THE PICTURES CHANGE AT THE SAME RATE. THEY NOW SHOW
VARIOUS ASPECTS OF HIS OFFICIAL AND PRIVATE LIFE. HE IS HAVING
DINNER WITH A GIRL, TYPING AT A TABLE IN HIS SHIRTSLEEVES,
WALKING DOWN THE STEPS OF AN AIRLINER, BUYING FRUIT AT A
STREET BARROW, SITTING IN A DECK CHAIR IN THE PARK READING,
WRITING A CHEQUE IN A BANK, ASLEEP IN BED, ENTERING HIS LON-
DON HOUSE AFTER HIS RESIGNATION. FINALLY, THERE IS A FULL FACE
PICTURE OF P WITH A FILE NUMBER UNDERNEATH.

NO. 2
You see, there isn't much we
don't know about you—but one
likes to know—everything. For
instance, I had no idea you
liked—lemon tea.

NO. 2 CHANGES THE PICTURE. WE NOW SEE P PLAYING CHESS WITH
A MAN WHO HAS A SMALL BEARD.

NO. 2
Also chess wasn't listed as one
of your hobbies. So you can't
be too careful, can you?

                              P
                    (THROWING DOWN THE FILE)
                    The time of my birth is missing.

                            NO. 2
                    There you are. There's another
                    thing. Now let's bring it all up
                    to date.

                              P
                    I've nothing to say. Is that clear?
                    Nothing.

                            NO. 2
                    Do be reasonable, old boy. It's
                    only a matter of time. Sooner
                    or later you'll tell me. Sooner
                    or later you'll want to. Let's make
                    a deal. You co-operate, tell us
                    what we want to know and this
                    can be a very nice place. You
                    may even be given a position
                    of authority.

                              P
                    I'm not making any deals with
                    you. I've resigned. I am not
                    going to be pushed, filed, in-
                    dexed, stamped, briefed, de-
                    briefed or numbered. My life is
                    my own.

                            NO. 2
                    Is it?

                              P
                    Yes. You won't hold me.

                            NO. 2
                    Won't we? Let me prove that we
                    will.

NO. 2 PUSHES A BUTTON AND GETS UP. A DOOR SLIDES OPEN AT
THE BACK OF THE LIVING SPACE.

                            NO. 2
                    (PICKING UP FILE) Come. I'll
                    show you. We can take this up
                    later.

P IS INTERESTED DESPITE HIMSELF. HE FOLLOWS NO. 2 THROUGH THE DOOR.

EXT. REAR AREA. DAY. LOC.   36

STANDING ON THE LAWN IS A HELICOPTER AND BESIDE IT IN THE ACT OF OPENING THE DOOR, THE BUTLER, WEARING SMART OVER-ALLS. THE HELICOPTER IS VERY MODERN. IT HAS NO NATIONAL MARK-INGS OR IDENTIFICATION INSIGNIA. P. STOPS.

                          NO. 2
                    After you.

THEY ENTER THE HELICOPTER. THE BLADES BEGIN TO ROTATE. THE BUTLER AT THE CONTROLS. THE 'COPTER LIFTS OFF.

INT. HELICOPTER. DAY.   37

PILOT IN FOREGROUND, MANIPULATING CONTROLS. P LOOKS OUT OF THE WINDOW, NO. 2 WATCHING HIM WITH A SLIGHT SMILE.

EXT. VILLAGE AND ENVIRONMENTS. DAY.   37A

THE VILLAGE LIES BENEATH LIKE A SMALL RELIEF MAP. IT IS SUR-ROUNDED BY FORESTS AND MOUNTAINS VISIBLY DEMONSTRATING ITS ISOLATION.

INT. HELICOPTER. DAY.   37B

                          NO. 2
                It's quite a beautiful place really,
                don't you think? Almost like a
                world on its own.

                           P
                I shall miss it when I've gone.

                          NO. 2
                Oh look. (HE POINTS) They're
                water skiing.

EXT. VILLAGE AND ENVIRONMENTS. DAY.   37C

A MOTOR BOAT IS TOWING A PAIR OF WATER SKIIERS.

INT. HELICOPTER. DAY.   37D

P SAYS NOTHING. HE IS TAKING IN THE LAY OUT.

                            NO. 2
                    It will grow on you. You'll find
                    we have everything here. In fact,
                    we're   completely   self-con-
                    tained. Water, electricity—oh,
                    that's our Council building.

EXT. VILLAGE AND ENVIRONMENTS. DAY.   37E

AERIAL SHOT OF TOWN HALL.

INT. HELICOPTER. DAY.   37F

                            NO. 2
                    We have our own Council.
                    Democratically elected. And we
                    also use it for film shows, pub-
                    lic meetings, amateur theatri-
                    cals.

                             P
                    Fascinating!

                            NO. 2
                    Then we have the cafe and our
                    general store—but of course
                    you know about that. But did
                    you know that we also have our
                    own little newspaper? The fel-
                    low who runs it was quite a bril-
                    liant journalist.

                             P
                    You must send me a copy.

                            NO. 2
                    (LAUGHS) Oh, capital. You'll be
                    the death of me.

THEY HOLD A LOOK.

                            NO. 2
                    (DEADLY) We also have our
                    own   graveyard.   (LIGHTLY
                    AGAIN, INDICATING BELOW)
                    But you'll be more interested
                    in the social club.

VILLAGE AND ENVIRONMENTS. DAY.   37G

AERIAL VIEW OF THE PLAY HOUSE.

INT. HELICOPTER. DAY.   37H

> NO. 2
> Members only. But I'll see what
> I can do for you.
>
> P
> You're too kind.
>
> NO. 2
> If you have any problems, there
> is our Citizens Advice Bureau.
> They do a marvellous job. Once
> you've settled in, it's not such
> a bad life. Everyone is very nice.
> You may even meet people you
> know.

P GIVES A SHARP LOOK AT NO. 2. NO. 2 TAPS THE PILOT ON THE
SHOULDER AND INDICATES THAT THEY SHOULD LAND.

EXT. BEACH. DAY. LOC.   38

WATER SKIIERS CROSSING FOREGROUND. THE HELICOPTER COMES
DOWN TO LAND ON THE GRASS STRIP BY THE SWIMMING POOL.
THERE ARE SEVERAL PEOPLE SWIMMING INCLUDING TWO OR THREE
ATTRACTIVE GIRLS. FIVE OR SIX OLDER PEOPLE ARE SITTING ON THE
TERRACE SUNNING THEMSELVES AND HAVING MORNING COFFEE.

EXT. HELICOPTER AND SWIMMING POOL. DAY.   38A

P COMES OUT FOLLOWED BY NO. 2, WHO IS STILL CARRYING THE
FILE. THEY BEGIN TO WALK FROM IT. NO. 2 INDICATING A COUPLE
OF ATTRACTIVE GIRLS SUNNING THEMSELVES.

> NO. 2
> As I said, it's not such a bad life.
> You'll soon feel at home.
>
> P
> What crime did they commit?
>
> NO. 2
> I'm glad your sense of humour
> is coming back.

NO. 2 NODS AT A MOCK SHIP BY THE SHORE. IT IS FIRMLY BEDDED
IN CONCRETE.

> NO. 2
> You'll probably see the funny
> side of that. I'm told some peo-
> ple even get seasick on it.

P IS NOT AMUSED. THEY WALK ON.

EXT. OLD PEOPLES' HOME. DAY.   38B
_____

PEOPLE ARE SITTING AROUND THE LAWN. THEY ARE VERY PLACID
AND SIT FACING THE SUN. NO. 2 AND P APPROACH.

> P
> Who are they?

> NO. 2
> They are the senior citizens.
> They have every comfort. You
> get looked after here for as long
> as you live.

> P
> They also made a big mistake.

NO. 2 AND P WALKING UP THE VILLAGE STREET.

> NO. 2
> They have very distinguished
> backgrounds. You see that old
> gentleman? Ex-admiral.

NO. 2 POINTS AT A WHITE-HAIRED MAN SITTING LIKE THE OTHERS
STARING INTO SPACE.

> NO. 2
> Excellent chess player.

P TAKES THIS IN.

> P
> I hope he finds a partner.

THE VILLAGE IS BY NOW IN FULL ACTIVITY. THE STREET IS BUSY.
FROM TIME TO TIME PASSERS-BY GIVE THAT ODD WAVE OF THE
HAND THAT COULD BE A SALUTE. NO. 2 ALWAYS RETURNS IT WITH
A GRACIOUS SMILE. APART FROM PEDESTRIAN TRAFFIC WE SEE IN
USE VARIOUS VEHICLES THAT ARE PART OF VILLAGE TRANSPORT. THE
"BEACH BUGGIES" WITH THEIR STRIPED CANOPIES ALREADY SEEN.

THE R.S.W. 16 BICYCLE. MINI TRACTORS SPEEDING AT TWO MILES AN HOUR. SOME OF THESE PULL TRAILERS.

TWO PEOPLE, A MAN AND A WOMAN, WALK PAST.

>   NO. 2
>   Good morning. Beautiful day.

>   THE COUPLE
>   (IN UNISON) Beautiful day.

>   NO. 2
>   (ALMOST CONSPIRATORIALLY
>   TO THE PRISONER) They didn't
>   settle for ages. Now they
>   wouldn't leave for the world.

>   P
>   You mean you brought them
>   round to your way of thinking.

>   NO. 2
>   (LOOKING O.S.) They had a
>   choice.

IN ONE OF THE TRACTOR DRAWN TRAILERS SITS A HANDSOME IN-TELLIGENT LOOKING MAN. HE IS FLYING A KITE. A PENNY FARTHING BICYCLE GOES BY. RIDING IT, AN ELDERLY MAN. HE GIVES THE WAVE TO NO. 2.

>   ELDERLY MAN
>   Be seeing you.

>   NO. 2
>   And you.

ALL VEHICLES HAVE STRIPED CANOPIES MATCHING THE "BUGGIES". ALL HAVE RADIO AERIALS.

SUDDENLY THE PICTURESQUE SCENE IS SHATTERED BY A SCREAMING SIREN NOT UNLIKE THAT OF AN AMBULANCE ON AN ERRAND OF DEATH. ALL MOVEMENT STOPS. THE VILLAGERS FREEZE IN THEIR TRACKS. NO. 2 ALSO. HE PUTS A FINGER TO HIS LIPS.

>   NO. 2
>   Wait.

P DOES SO. ALL IS VERY STILL. THE SIREN GROWS IN VOLUME. AROUND A CORNER HURTLES A VEHICLE AT GREAT SPEED. IT IS A LOW-SLUNG WHITE BEETLE-LIKE MACHINE. IT APPEARS TO BE WINDOWLESS AND

NO DRIVER IS IN EVIDENCE. IT LOOKS LIKE AN ELONGATED EGG WITH A BLUE FLASHING POLICE LIGHT ATOP. IT GOES TO THE END OF THE STREET, TURNS AND HURTLES BACK FROM WHERE IT CAME. PEACE RETURNS. THE VILLAGERS GO ABOUT THEIR BUSINESS AGAIN. NO. 2 MOVES OFF.

> P
> What was that?

> NO. 2
> "Rover".

> P
> "Rover" what?

> NO. 2
> Just "Rover".

> P
> Who drives it?

> NO. 2
> (WITH A PUZZLED LOOK)
> Drives it?

> P
> Yes. Who?

NO. 2 LAUGHS PLEASANTLY.

> NO. 2
> That would be telling.

EXT. OLD PEOPLES' HOME. DAY. LOC.   39

CLOSE SHOT OF LOUDSPEAKER. A SHORT SET SEQUENCE OF NOTES STRIKES.

> LOUDSPEAKER
> (AGAIN THAT MECHANICALLY
> CHEERFUL VOICE) Your atten-
> tion please. Here are two an-
> nouncements. Ice cream is now
> on sale for your enjoyment. The
> flavour of the day is strawberry.
> Here is a warning. (PAUSE)
> There is a possibility of light
> intermittent showers later in the
> day. Thank you for your atten-
> tion.

THE BACKGROUND MUSIC STARTS AGAIN.

EXT. OLD PEOPLES' HOME. DAY. LOC.   40

TWO SHOTS OF P AND NO. 2. IN THE BACKGROUND WE SEE TABLE
UMBRELLAS BEING OPENED FOR THE SENIOR CITIZENS BY WAITERS.
THE BACKGROUND MUSIC IS INTERRUPTED.

> LOUDSPEAKER
> Calling No. 2. Calling No. 2.
> Ready for you at Labour Ex-
> change.

> NO. 2
> Thank you. I'll be right there.

THE MUSIC RESTARTS. NO. 2 WALKS OFF. HE HAS SPOKEN IN A PER-
FECTLY NORMAL VOICE APPARENTLY TO THE AIR IN GENERAL. P REG-
ISTERS. NO. 2 CALLS BACK TO HIM.

> NO. 2
> Walk with me.

> P
> (GRIM) Why not?

> NO. 2
> (LAUGHS) Indeed.

THEY MOVE OFF.

EXT. GOLDFISH POND BY THE "ANGEL". DAY. LOC.   41

TWO MEN ARE ARGUING VIOLENTLY. THEY START TO FIGHT. TWO
GARDENERS WORKING AT A FLOWER BED ABOUT FIFTY YARDS AWAY
SUDDENLY DOWN TOOLS AND START RUNNING TOWARDS THE DIS-
TURBANCE. NO. 2 AND P APPEAR. THE TWO MEN FALL INTO THE
GOLDFISH POND AND ARE YANKED OUT BY THE GARDENERS WHO
MARCH THEM OFF, EXECUTING THE WHOLE OPERATION WITH THE
SKILL OF WELL-TRAINED POLICEMEN. THEY ARE FIRM BUT NOT BRU-
TAL.

> P
> What was that all about?

> NO. 2
> (IRRITATED BY THE EMBAR-
> RASSING SPECTACLE) Have you
> never seen two men fighting?

P
Yes, but they don't usually get
arrested by gardeners.

NO. 2
(IMPATIENTLY) P.M.C.'s Public
Minded Citizens. Now we really
must get to the Labour Exchange.

EXT. LABOUR EXCHANGE. DAY. LOC.   42

THEY GO INTO THE BUILDING.

INT. LABOUR EXCHANGE. DAY.   43

A MAN IS DOING PAPERWORK BEHIND THE COUNTER. AS NO. 2 AND
P ENTER, THE MAN STANDS UP.

MAN
Good morning, sir. Will you go
straight through.

THEY DO SO PASSING THROUGH A DOOR.

INT. MANAGER'S OFFICE. DAY.   44

THIS SET HAS THE SAME FUTURISTIC QUALITY AS NO. 2'S LIVING
SPACE. IT IS SET OUT FOR AN INTERVIEW. ON THE LARGE DESK ARE
JIG SAW PATTERNS. IN THE CENTRE ARE VARIOUS WOODEN SHAPES
OF DIFFERENT SIZES, AND DESIGNS. IT IS OBVIOUS THEY HAVE TO
BE INTERLINKED.

MANAGER
Ah, this is our new friend.
Everything is ready, sir. (TO P)
Please sit down.

P MAKES NO MOVE.

MANAGER
First of all, the aptitude test.

P, STILL STANDING, STARTS TO DO THE SIMPLE WOODEN BRICK TEST.
HE FINISHES WITH TWO PIECES OVER, ONE A RING, THE OTHER A
SQUARE PEG. THE MANAGER AND NO. 2 WATCH FOR HIS NEXT MOVE.
P WITHOUT LOOKING UP, SLOWLY PLACES THE SQUARE PEG ON TOP
OF THE ROUND HOLE. WITH A QUICK MOVE, HE DRIVES THE PEG
INTO THE HOLE WITH HIS FIST. NO. 2 AND THE MANAGER DO NOT
TURN A HAIR.

> MANAGER
> (HANDING P A FORM)
> And now the questionnaire. If
> you'd just fill in your race, your
> religion, your hobbies. What you
> like to read. What you like to
> eat. What you want to be. What
> were your and family diseases.
> Any politics?

P VIOLENTLY RIPS THE QUESTIONNAIRE INTO PIECES.

> NO. 2
> (TO MANAGER) Never mind.

HE PASSES P'S PERSONAL FILE OVER.

> NO. 2
> You can get all you need from
> this.

P EXPLODES. WITH HIS WOODEN "HAMMER" HE SMASHES ALL THE
PARAPHERNALIA ON THE DESK. HE SLAMS OUT LEAVING A SHAMBLES
BEHIND.

> NO. 2
> I think we have a challenge.

> *FADE OUT:*

> *END OF ACT TWO*

Number Six's Campaign Speech
From "Free for All"

EXT. BALCONY. DAY. LOC.   24

CHEERS. SUBSIDE. SILENCE. P EYES THEM.

> P
> At some time, in some place, all
> of you held positions of a secret
> nature and had knowledge in-
> valuable to an enemy. Like me,
> you are here, either to have that
> knowledge protected or ex-
> tracted.

EXT. VILLAGE. DAY. LOC.   25

THE CROWD. BECOMING EXCITED. CHEERS. THE DRUM. CYMBALS.

EXT. BALCONY. DAY. LOC.   26

P LOOKS AT NO. 2 WHO NODS WITH A HARD TIGHT SMILE.

> NO. 2
> That's the stuff to give 'em.

P TURNS AGAIN TO THE CROWD. HE SHOUTS THEM INTO SILENCE.

> P
> Unlike me, many of you have
> accepted the situation of your
> imprisonment and will die here
> like rotten cabbages.

EXT. VILLAGE. DAY. LOC.   27

THE CROWD STANDS IN SHOCK. DEAD SILENCE.

EXT. BALCONY. DAY. LOC.   28

NO. 2 MOVES CLOSE TO P.

> NO. 2
> (whispered)
> Keep going. They're loving it.

> P
> The rest of you have gone over
> to the side of our Keepers.
> Which is which? How many of
> each? Who's standing beside you
> now?

EXT. VILLAGE. DAY. LOC.   29

CROWD, ALMOST IMPERCEPTIBLY EACH PERSON APPEARS ISOLATED.
THEY NEVER TAKE THEIR EYES FROM THE BALCONY. THE TWO PUBLIC
MINDED CITIZENS WHO WERE HOLDING THE PENNY-FARTHING UP-
RIGHT NO LONGER SUPPORT IT. THE OLD MAN HAS A JOB TO MAIN-
TAIN BALANCE. HE SPRINTS THE BICYCLE A FEW FURIOUS YARDS TO
A TREE AND LEANS AGAINST THAT.

EXT. BALCONY. DAY. LOC.   30

CLOSE SHOT OF P.

P

I intend to discover who are the
Prisoners and who the Warders. (pause) *I shall be running
for Office in this Election.*

HE MOVES FROM THE MICROPHONE. NO. 2 IMMEDIATELY TAKES OVER.

NO. 2

Good people, let us applaud a
citizen of character. May the
better man win and a big hand
for No. 6.

Number Six's Encounter with Mrs. Butterworth
From "Many Happy Returns"

INT. P'S KITCHEN (LONDON) DAY.   147

HE COMES IN. IT IS TIDY AND FAMILIAR. UNTIL HE NOTICES THE
FLORAL TEAPOT ON THE TABLE. HE OPENS THE HIGH WALL-CUP-
BOARD. THE CHINA IN HERE IS ALSO PRETTILY FLORAL. HE SHUTS IT
AND TURNS. AN EMPTY SAUCEPAN STANDS ON THE GAS STOVE. HE
TAKES IT UP AND LOOKS AT IT. IT IS NOT ONE OF HIS. THEN HE
GOES TO THE FRIDGE, OPENS IT AND TAKES OUT THE REMAINS OF
A CHICKEN. HE BRINGS IT TO THE TABLE, PULLS OFF A LEG AND
CHEWS RAVENOUSLY AT IT AS HE LOOKS ABOUT AGAIN, TAKING IN
THE DETAILS. HE STOPS CHEWING AS HE HEARS THE FRONT DOOR
OPEN AND SHUT. HE MOVES QUICKLY BEHIND THE DOOR. THE DOOR
IS OPENED AND SOMEONE SURVEYS THE ROOM. WITH A QUICK GRAB
OF THE DOOR, P PULLS IT WIDE TO GRAB THE INTRUDER. A LITTLE
OLD LADY.

MRS. BUTTERWORTH

No! Don't you touch me! Who
are you? (HE JUST LOOKS AT
HER) Are you a burglar?

P

Are you?

MRS. BUTTERWORTH

Don't be impertinent. (OF THE
CHICKEN) That's my dinner
you're eating.

                                   P
                    In my fridge?

                    MRS. BUTTERWORTH
                    If you're not a burglar, you're
                    a lunatic. I'm not afraid of you.
                    (SHE BEGINS TO GET ANGRY)
                    The very idea!

SHE TURNS AND MARCHES AWAY.

INT. P'S LIVING ROOM (LONDON) DAY.   148

TO THE TELEPHONE. P FOLLOWS HER TO THE DOORWAY, WATCHES
AS SHE DIALS 999.

                    MRS. BUTTERWORTH
                    Bursting in here! I'll soon deal
                    with you, my lad.

                                   P
                    It's my flat.

                    VOICE OF OPERATOR
                    Emergency. Which service do
                    you require?

HE MOVES TO HER.

                                   P
                    My *flat*! I live here!

SHE LOOKS UP AT HIM.

                    VOICE OF OPERATOR
                    Emergency. Which service do
                    you require? Hallo?

SHE PUTS THE TELEPHONE DOWN.

                    MRS. BUTTERWORTH
                    I can ring again. And shall. You
                    do not live here. I have a lease.

                                   P
                    Who from?

                    MRS. BUTTERWORTH
                    The estate-agent, of course. Who
                    are you? What do you want?

P
(LOOKS ABOUT) I lived here.
I still own it.

MRS. BUTTERWORTH
(DOUBTFULLY) You don't
sound like a burglar.

P
How long have you been here?

MRS. BUTTERWORTH
Several weeks. *I* should be asking *you* questions.

HE TAKES UP THE TELEPHONE AND DIALS.

P
We'll ask the agent. See where
he got his instructions.

MRS. BUTTERWORTH
It's Saturday afternoon. He won't
be there.

THE NUMBER RINGS. NO ANSWER. HE PUTS THE TELEPHONE DOWN.

MRS. BUTTERWORTH
You can't do anything till Mon-
day. Can you prove you lived
here?

P
I doubt it. (LOOKS AT HER)
What month is it?

MRS. BUTTERWORTH
March. Are you all right?

P
(REALISING) Then I'm sorry. I
owe you an apology. My lease
has run out. They didn't waste
much time.

HE GOES TO THE FRONT DOOR, LOOKS BACK.

P
Are any of my things here? I'd
like to change.

> MRS. BUTTERWORTH
No.

HE DOES LOOK A BIT DEFEATED.

> MRS. BUTTERWORTH
> Would you like some tea?

> P
> I must get on. You wouldn't
> know where they are? Where
> they've been stored?

> MRS. BUTTERWORTH
> I've no idea. I'll make that tea.

HE WATCHES HER TO THE OTHER DOOR. SHE LOOKS BACK.

> MRS. BUTTERWORTH
> Though I did find a suitcase. In
> the cupboard under the stairs.
> Shall I fetch it?

> P
> I will. (THEN—) I know where
> it is.

> MRS. BUTTERWORTH
> (WATCHING HIM) No one's
> ever asked after you.

> P
> (AT THE FRONT DOOR) That
> would have been arranged.

MRS. BUTTERWORTH GOES OUT. P GOES OUT OF THE FRONT DOOR
TO THE PASSAGE.

EXT. P'S KITCHEN (LONDON) DAY.   149

MRS. BUTTERWORTH COMES IN. SHE IS WORRIED, BUT MAKES UP
HER MIND AND FILLS THE KETTLE AT THE TAP.

DISSOLVE:

INT. P'S LIVING ROOM (LONDON) DAY.   150

THE REMAINS OF TEA AND SANDWICHES ON THE TABLE. MRS. BUT-
TERWORTH. DRINKING HER SECOND CUP, LOOKS UP AS P COMES
FROM THE BATHROOM IN HIS OFFICE CLOTHES, CLEAN AND SHAVED.

P
My second-best suit.

MRS. BUTTERWORTH
I liked the beard.

P NOTICES A LITTLE SILVER CALENDAR ON THE BUREAU AND TAKES IT UP.

P
March the eighteenth?

MRS. BUTTERWORTH
If that's what it says.

P
Then tomorrow's my birthday.

HE JOINS HER.

P
Thanks for the food. I'm sorry I gave you a fright.

MRS. BUTTERWORTH
Only a little one. (SHE SIPS HER TEA) My son would be about your age.

P
Would?

MRS. BUTTERWORTH
He died. Where will you stay? There's the sofa.

P
I won't trouble you. I have some "friends".

MRS. BUTTERWORTH
(SLIGHTLY EMBARRASSED) Are you all right for money? (HE IS TOUCHED) I could lend you a little.

P
I'll go to the bank.

MRS. BUTTERWORTH
It's Saturday.

                        P
    So it is.

            MRS. BUTTERWORTH
    You're a funny man. You really
    did live here? It's not a fib?

                        P
    I swear it. Now I must be on
    my way.

            MRS. BUTTERWORTH
    (RISING) So soon?

                        P
    I'll come back. To thank you
    properly.

SHE FOLLOWS HIM TO THE DOOR.

            MRS. BUTTERWORTH
    If you come back tomorrow, I'll
    make you a birthday cake.

                        P
    I had a cat. I suppose that's gone
    too.

            MRS. BUTTERWORTH
    They gave me the key to a ga-
    rage. Said it went with the flat.

HE WATCHES HER TO THE BUREAU WHERE SHE FUMBLES IN A DRAWER.

            MRS. BUTTERWORTH
    I've never been near it

SHE RETURNS WITH THE TAGGED KEY.

                        P
    Thank you.

HE OPENS THE FRONT DOOR.

            MRS. BUTTERWORTH
    You'll try to come back?

                        P
    I promise. I'm sure you make
    wonderful cakes.

HE GOES AND SHUTS THE DOOR.

Number Six Breaks Number Two
From "Hammer into Anvil"

INT. NO. 2'S LIVING SPACE. DAY.   185

NO. 2 IS SITTING CURLED UP IN THE EGG-CHAIR LIKE A FOETUS IN
THE WOMB. HE LOOKS UP OPEN-MOUTHED AS P COMES IN. P COMES
DOWN THE RAMP TO THE DESK. AT LAST NO. 2 MANAGES TO SAY:

> NO. 2
> What are you doing here?

> P
> Keeping you company. I hear
> all your friends have deserted
> you. You can't really trust any-
> one, can you? Pity.

P MAKES A WIDE SWEEPING GESTURE WITH HIS HAND ROUND THE
LIVING SPACE.

> P
> It's odd isn't it? All this power
> at your disposal—and yet you're
> alone. You do feel that, don't
> you? Alone?

NO. 2 LOOKS AT HIM UNCERTAINLY. VERY MUCH ON THE DEFENSIVE.

> NO. 2
> What do you want?

P STARTS TO WALK ROUND THE DESK.

> P
> To talk and to listen.

P IS BEHIND NO. 2'S CHAIR NOW. NO. 2 DOES NOT SWIVEL ROUND.

> NO. 2
> (MUTTERS) I have nothing to
> say.

P SPINS THE CHAIR ROUND SO THAT NO. 2 IS FACING HIM.

> P
> Oh come now. That doesn't
> sound like No. 2. What's hap-
> pened to the strong man? The

hammer. "You must either be
a hammer or an anvil." Remember?

NO. 2 CAN NO LONGER LOOK HIM IN THE EYE. HE IS STRUGGLING
WITH HIMSELF. AT LAST THE WORDS FORCE THEMSELVES OUT.

NO. 2
I know who you are.

P COMES ROUND TO THE SIDE OF HIS CHAIR.

P
I'm No. 6.

NO. 2
(IN A BURST) No!—D.6.

P
D.6?

NO. 2
Sent here by our Masters! To
spy on me!

P
I'm not with you.

NO. 2
Oh, yes! You can stop acting
now. I was on to you from the
beginning. I knew what was
going on.

P
Tell me.

NO. 2
All those messages you sent. And
the people you recruited. I knew
you were a plant. You didn't fool
me.

P
Perhaps—you fooled yourself.

NO. 2
(BEAT) What does that mean?

P
Let us suppose—for the sake of
argument—that what you say is
true. That I was planted here.

NO. 2
By X.O.4.

P
X.O.4? Very well. X.O.4. to check
on the village security. To check
on you . . .

NO. 2
You were.

P
Then in that case what would
your duty be—as a loyal citizen?

NO. 2 STARES AT P IN GROWING FEAR AS THE MEANING OF WHAT P
IS SAYING BEGINS TO DAWN ON HIM.

P
Not to interfere. But you did.
You've admitted it yourself.
There's a name for that—sab-
otage!

NO. 2 STARTS UP OUT OF THE CHAIR.

NO. 2
(FRANTICALLY) No!

P LEANS ACROSS THE DESK. THE WORDS COME OUT LIKE BULLETS.

P
*Who are you working for, No.
2?*

NO. 2
(WILDLY) For us! For us!

P
Are you? That isn't how it would
look to—X.O.4.

NO. 2 COMES ROUND THE DESK. HIS HANDS OUT. IMPLORING.

NO. 2
I swear to you ...

P
You could be working for the
enemy. Or you could be a bun-
gler who lost his head. Either
way, you've failed. And they
don't like failure here.

NO. 2
(DULLY) You've ... destroyed
... me.

P
No. You destroyed yourself. A
character flaw—you feared your
Masters. A weak link in the chain
of command—waiting to be
broken.

NO. 2 FALLS TO HIS KNEES IN A PANIC.

NO. 2
Don't tell them! Don't report me!

P
I don't intend to.

A LONG SHUDDERING SIGH ESCAPES NO. 2. HE SOBS WITH RELIEF.

P
(ALL ICE) You are going to report yourself.

NO. 2 LOOKS UP AT HIM WITH GLAZED EYES. HE SEEMS PARALYSED.
P TAKES THE PHONE OFF THE DESK AND PUTS IT IN NO. 2'S NERVE-
LESS FINGERS. NO. 2 SPEAKS IN A FLAT MECHANICAL VOICE.

NO. 2
(AS IN A TRANCE) I am re-
porting a breakdown in control. No. 2 will need to be
replaced ... Yes, this is No. 2
reporting.

THE PHONE SLIPS FROM HIS HAND TO THE FLOOR. P LOOKS DOWN
AT THE CRUMPLED FIGURE WITHOUT PITY. NO. 2 IS MORE PUPPET
THAN MAN. P GOES UP THE RAMP, LOOKS BACK. NO. 2 REMAINS

SLUMPED ON THE FLOOR, STARING INTO SPACE. IT IS FINISHED. HAMMER INTO ANVIL. P GOES THROUGH SLIDING DOORS.

Degree Absolute, The Embryo Room, and The Cage
From "Once Upon a Time"

THE CAGE. IT IS EMPTY. THE DOOR AJAR. PULL BACK. ANGELO IS AT THE ELECTRIC ORGAN. HE PLAYS A LULLABY. PULL BACK MORE. NO. 2 IS LYING ON THE TABLE CENTRE. P WALKS AROUND HIM.

P
You chose this method because you know the only way to beat me was to gain my respect?

NO. 2
That is correct.

P
And then I would confide.

NO. 2
I hoped that you would come to trust me.

P
It is a recognised method?

NO. 2
Used in psychoanalysis. The patient must come to trust his doctor totally.

P
Sometimes they change places.

NO. 2
It is essential in extreme cases.

P
Also a risk?

NO. 2
A grave risk.

P
If the doctor has his own problems.

NO. 2
I have.

P
And that is why your system is
called Degree Absolute?

NO. 2
It's one or the other of us.

P
Why don't you resign?

NO. 2 SITS UP. LOOKS AT P. HE LAUGHS HEARTILY.

NO. 2
Very good. You're very good at
it.

HE GETS OFF THE TABLE. TALKS AT ANGELO.

NO. 2
Play something cheerful!

ANGELO DOES SO. NO. 2 GOES INTO THE CAGE. OPENS THE RE-
FRIGERATOR. TAKES OUT A BOTTLE.

P
I'd like to know more.

NO. 2
You'll have every opportunity
before we're through.

HE TAKES TWO GLASSES AND THE BOTTLE TO THE TABLE.

NO. 2
Join me.

P
Straight?

NO. 2
One hundred percent.

HE FILLS THE TWO GLASSES. HANDS ONE TO P.

P
No additions?

HE RAISES HIS GLASS. EXAMINES IT. NO. 2 ALSO.

NO. 2
My word of honour.

THEY EYE EACH OTHER.

P
Cheers.

THEY DRINK.

P
Mind if I inspect our home from home?

THEY WANDER AMIABLY ABOUT THE ROOM.

NO. 2
This desirable residence is known as the "Embryo Room". In it you can relive from the cradle to the grave. There is no way out until our time is up. If we can solve our mutual problem, that will be forty-eight hours approximately from now.

P RAISES A SECTION OF BLACK CURTAIN. STEEL WALL BEHIND.

NO. 2
You can take my word for it.

P
Naturally I would.

HE RAISES ANOTHER SECTION. STEEL WALL. NO. 2 SMILES.

NO. 2
Let me show you to the door.

HE MOVES OVER TO A FURTHER SECTION. PULLS A CORD. THE STEEL DOOR IS REVEALED.

NO. 2
We are protected from intruders in a most efficient way. No one shall interrupt our, shall I say, deliberations?

HE BANGS A FIST AGAINST THE STEEL.

>   NO. 2
>   Entirely encased in finest steel.

HE PULLS A CORD AND THE CLOCK IS REVEALED.

>   NO. 2
>   Behold the clock.

HE LOOKS AT IT. THE DIAL MOVES. HE PANICS.

>   NO. 2
>   Five minutes! Set to open in a
>   new phase of our relationship.
>   That is, if we're still here.

>   P
>   Are we likely to move?

>   NO. 2
>   It's possible.

>   P
>   Somewhere nice?

NO. 2 MOVES TO THE CAGE.

>   P
>   Built in bars?

>   NO. 2
>   Also self-contained.

HE GOES INTO THE CAGE. DEMONSTRATES. WILDLY.

>   NO. 2
>   Bathroom. Kitchen. Air-condi-
>   tioning. Food supplies for six
>   months. You could go any-
>   where in it. It even has a waste-
>   disposal unit.

P EXPERIMENTS WITH THE DOOR FROM THE OUTSIDE. CLOSES IT.
REFERRING TO "CAGE".

>   P
>   It moves?

>   NO. 2
>   It's detachable.

P OPENS THE DOOR. CLOSES IT. LOCKS IT. TAKES OUT THE KEY.

                            P
                 What's behind it?

NO. 2 LOOKS AT HIM. AND AT THE LOCKED DOOR.

                         NO. 2
                 Steel.

INT. EMBRYO ROOM. SECTION.   29

ANGELO AT THE ORGAN. HE STOPS PLAYING. HE MOVES ACROSS THE
ROOM TO P. HE STANDS BESIDE HIM. HE BOWS AT P.

INT. EMBRYO ROOM CAGE.   30

NO. 2 WATCHES IN FEAR.

                         NO. 2
                 He thinks you're the boss now.

                            P
                 I am.

                         NO. 2
                 You're not. Give him the key.

                            P
                 No.

                         NO. 2
                 Give him the key!

                            P
                 Why?

                         NO. 2
                 I'm No. 2. The boss. Give him
                 the key.

                            P
                 No. One is the boss.

                         NO. 2
                 No.

                            P
                 No?

                         NO. 2
                 No. Three minutes. I'm the boss.

                              P
              Three minutes. You're scared.

                           NO. 2
              No!

                              P
              You can't take it.

                           NO. 2
              Fool!

                              P
              Yes. Not a rat.

                           NO. 2
              You're scared.

                              P
              Want me to come in?

                           NO. 2
              Keep out.

                              P
              Let you out?

                           NO. 2
              Stay away.

                              P
              I'll come in.

                           NO. 2
              Get out.

                              P
              You're mine.

P SIGNALS TO ANGELO. HANDS HIM THE KEY TO THE CAGE. ANGELO
GOES TO OPEN THE DOOR.

                           NO. 2
              Stop him.

                              P
              Two minutes.

ANGELO HAS UNLOCKED THE DOOR. NUMBER TWO STANDS BEFORE
THE OPEN DOOR. ANGELO BOWS.

P

Come out.

NO. 2

No.

P

The door is open.

NO. 2

No!

P

You're free.

NO. 2

I'm No. 2.

P

One minute, thirty-five seconds.

NO. 2

Why did you resign?

P

Why did you accept?

NO. 2

You resigned.

P

I don't accept.

NO. 2

You accepted before you resigned.

P

I rejected.

NO. 2

Who?

P ENTERS THE CAGE, CONFRONTS NUMBER TWO.

P

You.

NO. 2

Why me?

                              P
          You're big.

NO. 2 BACKS AWAY FROM HIM WITHIN THE CAGE.

                         No. 2
          Not tall.

                              P
          Not tall.

                         No. 2
          That's right.

                              P
          Big.

                         No. 2
          Yes.

                              P
          Humpty Dumpty.

                         No. 2
          All the king's horses.

                              P
          That's right.

                         No. 2
          Couldn't put Humpty . . .

                              P
          And all the king's men.

                         No. 2
          What?

                              P
          Couldn't put Humpty together
          again.

                         No. 2
          A minute to go.

                              P
          Fifty-nine seconds.

                         No. 2
          I'm big.

P

Fifty-eight.

No. 2

You're tall.

P

Fifty-seven.

No. 2

Not small.

P

Fifty-six.

No. 2

Be glad.

P

Fifty-five.

No. 2

Thank God.

P

Who? Fifty four.

No. 2

God.

P

Fifty-three.

No. 2

Not for me.

P

Fifty-two.

No. 2

I'm for you.

P

Fifty-one.

No. 2

Resign.

P

Fifty.

No. 2

Tell me.

P

Forty-nine.

No. 2

Why resign?

P

Forty-eight.

No. 2

Don't resign.

P

Forty-seven.

No. 2

Tell me.

P

Forty-six.

No. 2

You know . . .

P

Forty-five.

No. 2

You know why . . .

P

Forty-four.

No. 2

Why did you?

P

Forty-three.

P WALKS FROM THE CAGE. HE CIRCLES THE ROOM SLOWLY. NO. 2
FOLLOWS HIM. P IS HEADING FOR THE CLOCK.

No. 2

You're for me.

P

Forty-two.

No. 2

I'm for you.

P

Forty-one.

No. 2

Ask me.

P

Forty.

No. 2

Easy.

P

Thirty-nine.

No. 2

Ask me.

P

Thirty-eight.

No. 2

I'll tell.

P

Thirty-seven.

No. 2

Anything.

P

Thirty-six.

No. 2

Not too late.

P

Thirty-five.

THEY ARRIVE BESIDE THE CLOCK. IT TICKS AWAY.

No. 2

Not too late.

P

For me?

No. 2

For me!

P

You snivel and grovel.

No. 2

I ask.

P

You crawl.

No. 2

Yes.

P

To ask?

No. 2

Yes.

P

Why?

No. 2

To know.

P

Ask on. Ask yourself.

No. 2

Why? Why?

P MOVES FROM THE CLOCK BACK TO THE CAGE. NO. 2 RUNS AHEAD
OF HIM INTO THE CAGE. P REMAINS WITHOUT.

P

Fifteen.

No. 2

Please.

P

Don't say please.

No. 2

I say it.

P

Don't

No. 2

Please, I plead.

P

Nine.

No. 2

Too late.

	P
Eight	
	No. 2.
I'll die.	
	P
Die!	
	No. 2
Seven.	
	P
Die!	
	No. 2
Six.	
	P
Die! Six. Die!	
	No. 2
Five.	
	P
Die!	
	No. 2
Four.	
	P
Die!	
	No. 2
Three.	
	P
Die!	
	No. 2
Two.	
	P
Die!	
	No. 2
One.	
	P
Die!	
	No. 2
Zero.	

>   P
> Die!

>   No. 2
> Zero.

HE DIES. THE CLOCK ALARMS. THE STEEL DOORS OPEN. INSIDE STANDS THE SUPERVISOR. ANGELO CLOSES THE CAGE.

>   SUPERVISOR
> Congratulations.

HE PRESSES A SWITCH ON THE CLOCK. A HINGED FRONT FALLS FROM ABOVE TO ENCLOSE THE CAGE.

>   SUPERVISOR
> We shall need the body for evi-
> dence. What do you desire?

>   P
> Number One.

>   SUPERVISOR
> I'll take you.

ANGELO LEADS THE WAY. THE SUPERVISOR GESTURES FOR P TO FOLLOW HIM. THEY MOVE INTO THE SUBTERRANEAN CORRIDOR. TRACK INTO THE FRONT OF THE CAGE. WE HEAR A SOUND, LOUD, AND GROWING IN VOLUME—AS OF A ROCKET LAUNCHING.

Number Six Meets Number One
From "Fall Out"

INT. THE CHAMBER. DAY.   84

THE PRESIDENT.

>   PRESIDENT
> Sir, on behalf of us all—we
> thank you. And now I take it that
> you are prepared to meet No.
> 1, sir?

P SAYS NOTHING.

>   PRESIDENT
> Follow me if you would be so
> kind, sir.

INT. THE CHAMBER. DAY.   85

THE PRESIDENT WALKS THE LENGTH OF THE CHAMBER. P DOES NOT MOVE. THE PRESIDENT STOPS BESIDE THE "LIFE POD" ADJACENT TO THE SEE-SAW.

INT. THE CHAMBER. DAY.   86

ALL IS STILL. P LEAVES THE PRESIDENT'S DAIS. CROSS THE CHAMBER. MOUNTS THE "POD". IT DESCENDS. P SINKS FROM VIEW.

INT. THE CHAMBER. DAY.   87

FROM ABOVE WE SEE P DESCENDING.

INT. LIFT SHAFT. DAY.   88

FROM BELOW WE SEE P DESCENDING.

INT. BASE OF LIFT SHAFT DAY.   89

THE POD COMES TO REST.

CLOSE SHOT. P.   90

LOOKING. HE MOVES OUT.

INT. CORRIDOR. DAY.   91

CLINICAL. METALLIC. LINES ON BOTH SIDES WITH WHITE-HELMETED GUARDS. THEY CARRY TOMMY GUNS, AT THE FAR END A STEEL DOOR. IT SLIDES OPEN, BEYOND CAN BE SEEN THE CIRCULAR INTERIOR OF THE "SENTENCE" ROOM. ALSO REVEALED THE YOUNG MAN AND NO. 2.

ENCASED IN CYLINDRICAL PERSPEX CONES. THEY ARE MARKED "ORBIT 48" AND "ORBIT 2". BESIDE THEM IS ANOTHER MARKED "ORBIT"—IT IS EMPTY. THE YOUNG MAN SINGS TO HIMSELF. NO. 2 LAUGHS TO HIMSELF. WE CANNOT HEAR EITHER OF THEM.

INT. SENTENCE ROOM. DAY.   92

P ENTERS. VAPOURS AS AT THE BASE OF THE ROCKET INHABIT THE ATMOSPHERE. A SPIRAL STAIRCASE LEADS UP. FOUR MASKED AND SHROUDED FIGURES AT ATTENTION. ANOTHER AT A CONTROL PANEL MANIPULATING DIALS. P HEARS A NOISE. TURNS. SEES:

INT. CORRIDOR. DAY. 93

THE "LIFT POD" DESCENDING, BUTLER ABOARD. THE "POD" COMES TO REST. THE BUTLER WALKS THE LENGTH OF THE CORRIDOR.

INT. SENTENCE ROOM. DAY. 94

THE BUTLER ENTERING, STEEL DOOR CLOSES BEHIND HIM. HE GOES TO THE BASE OF THE SPIRAL STAIRCASE. HE BOWS TO P AND INDICATES FOR HIM TO CLIMB. P MOVES FORWARD AND TAKES THE FIRST STEP.

INT. SENTENCE ROOM. DAY. 95

FROM ABOVE WE SEE P CLIMBING THE STAIRCASE.

INT. "ONE" ROOM. DAY. 96

P ENTERING AT THE TOP OF THE SPIRAL STAIRCASE. HE SEES:

INT. "ONE" ROOM. DAY. 97

A CYLINDRICAL METALLIC ROOM. IT IS FESTOONED WITH GLOBES OF THE WORLD, ALL SIZES. AT A CONTROL PANEL—A SHROUDED MASKED FIGURE. HIS BACK TO P. IN HIS HANDS A FORTUNE TELLER'S CRYSTAL BALL. IN FRONT OF HIM A SMALL SCREEN. ON SCREEN WE CAN SEE P'S ARRIVAL IN THE ROOM. A DOOR SLIDES TO BEHIND HIM.

THE FIGURE DOES NOT MOVE. P GOES FORWARD. HE STANDS BEHIND THE FIGURE. ON SCREEN THE IMAGE CHANGES TO A CLOSE-UP OF P OUT OF THE FIRST EPISODE SAYING:

P

I am not going to be pushed,
filed, indexed, stamped, briefed,
debriefed or numbered. My life
is my own.

THE FIGURE SLOWLY TURNS. ON FRONT OF ITS SHROUD IS MARKED THE NUMBER 1. IT RAISES THE CRYSTAL BALL TO P. ON SCREEN P'S IMAGE STILL HELD IN CLOSE UP REPEATS THE FIRST WORD LIKE A STUCK RECORD.

P

I-I-I-I . . .

CLOSE SHOT P. 98

REACTING

THE "ONE" ROOM. DAY.   99

THE FIGURE IS PRESENTING THE CRYSTAL BALL. P TAKES IT. HE LOOKS. THROUGH IT WE SEE THE DISTORTED MASK OF NO. 1. IT ECHOES WITH HOLLOW LAUGHTER. P REACHES OUT AND WRENCHES THE MASK AWAY.

BENEATH IS THE CHATTERING HEAD OF A CHIMPANZEE. P REACHES AGAIN AND REMOVES THE HEAD. BEHIND IS HIS OWN FACE. BESTIAL IN EXPRESSION. CHATTERING ALSO.

INT. "ONE" ROOM. DAY.   100

THE CRYSTAL BALL SHATTERS ON THE FLOOR.

INT. "ONE" ROOM. DAY.   101

LAUGHTER CONTINUES. ON SCREEN THE IMAGE REPEATS. P GOES BERSERK. HE FIGHTS WITH NO. 1. IT IS INTENSELY VIOLENT. SEEMINGLY BETWEEN MAN AND A BEAST. THE FACE WITHIN THE SHROUD IS NEVER SEEN AGAIN. THE FIGHT CULMINATES WITH NO. 1 ESCAPING UP A STEEL LADDER. P FOLLOWS HIM. AT THE TOP OF THE LADDER A CIRCULAR STEEL DOOR SLAMS SHUT. THERE IS A LOCKING DEVICE ON ITS LOWER SIDE. P SPINS IT AND DESCENDS THE LADDER.